Praise for *Mountain Time*

Renata Golden's *Mountain Time: A Field Guide to Astonishment* would be at home with Annie Dillard's *Pilgrim at Tinker Creek*, or Edward Abbey's *Desert Solitaire*. Or, best, with Robin Wall Kimmerer's *Braiding Sweetgrass*, for humility and listening and deep awareness of multiple stories and voices. But these gemlike sentences are Golden's own, and they woo me into an affair with a place I've never been. Fierce and beguiling, funny and brave, this is a book about love: how to love a place where you find yourself a visitor, and how to love the life you've won for yourself.

—**Joni Tevis**, author of *The World Is On Fire*

In this luminous collection, Renata Golden offers us an un-easy love story: with birds and people, mountains and family, history and place. Elegantly researched and exquisitely crafted, these essays have a depth and range that will delight and, yes, astonish.

—**Susan Fox Rogers**, author of *Learning the Birds, Editor of When Birds Are Near*

With a wonderful mix of history, memory, observation, imagination, and wit, Renata Golden leads us into a landscape that is both stark in its harshness and delightful in it details. Mountain Time reaches from the personal to the universal, opening our eyes, refreshing our senses, and making a home in our hearts. It's an absorbing book, a remarkably good read.

—**Gregory Nobles**, author of *John James Audubon: The Nature of the American Woodsman*

T0000430

With her thought-provoking debut essay collection, *Mountain Time: A Field Guide to Astonishment*, Renata Golden grounds us in place and explores transformative relationships with the human and nonhuman community of the Chiricahuas. Golden encounters longtime ranchers and newcomers like herself, prairie dogs, leopard frogs, snakes, bluebirds, ants, and a special greyhound. She explores what it means to call a place home while thoughtfully considering the conflict between the US Government and the Chiricahua Apaches, the people indigenous to the area. Throughout the collection attentiveness, time passed in a place deeply observing, is reverence. These transporting essays, at times open and vulnerable—which makes them right but not self-righteous—take us on journeys of thought and emotion. The way travel gives one perspective to see home through a new lens upon one's return, these essays will give you a new lens to see the world, and you'll be grateful for that.

—**Sean Hill**, author of *Blood Ties & Brown Liquor* and *Dangerous Goods*

This is a wonderful book. Renata Golden writes with the passion of Edward Abbey and the heart of Thoreau.

—**Bill Cavaliere**, President, Cochise County Historical Society and author of *The Chiricahua Apaches: A Concise History*

Renata Golden

MOUNTAIN TIME
A Field Guide to Astonishment

Columbus State University
PRESS
COLUMBUS, GEORGIA

Copyright © Renata Golden 2024
All rights reserved. No part of this book may be reproduced or transmitted
in any form or by any means electronic or mechanical including photocopying
recording or any information storage and retrieval system without permission
in writing from the Publisher.

Library of Congress Control Number: 2023942182

ISBN 9798988732129 (paperback)
ISBN 9798988732136 (epub)
ISBN 9798988732167 (PDF)

Published by Columbus State University Press

Marketing and distribution by UGA Press

Cover designed by Peter Selgin | Cover photo by Thomas Duncan

Author photo by Rose Abela

For Keith and for all who have lived on this land

Contents

Mountain Time

*"God doesn't need to come down upon a mountain, for the mountain
itself is the revelation. We only have to look at it and we will know
how we should live."*

John Moriarty

Researchers with seismometers and good climbing shoes have
found that mountains vibrate with a rhythm that keeps time, like
a breath. Mountains amplify the internal energy that rises from deep
within the earth in a subtle response to changes they experience around
them, including earthquakes and other traumas. The researchers
concluded that the mountains' constant hum associates their external
changes with internal damage. Over time, the mountains arrive at their
own conclusions. I'm still here, their heartbeats affirm. I'm alive.

I climb to the top of the mounds behind the house in Sulphur Canyon
where I once lived, more than a decade ago, on and off for three
years. The motives for my unlikely move here as well as my reasons
for leaving remain hidden to me, buried like the deep layers of lava
flows and faulting that color these cliffs. When I return, I hear the
mountains speaking to me in a tone I can't ignore, a voice humming
with suggestion. The Chiricahua Mountains, which have seen countless
sunrises and sunsets, which change their appearance based on the time
of day, seasons, and my point of view, speak of eternal change. They
remind me that there are many ways of knowing.

Irish poet and philosopher John O'Donohue has said that "One of the wonderful insights of the Celtic imagination is that landscape is alive." Perhaps I inherited that imagination from my grandmother, an Irish immigrant who never saw these mountains, but surely would have felt their heartbeat. She arrived at Ellis Island at the height of Irish immigration after *An Gorta Mór*, the Great Hunger, when a years-long blight decimated the potato crop. I try to live inside her dreams as she voyaged to America. In the mountainless landscape of Chicago, what held my grandmother's secrets? She moved from rural Ireland to South Side streets; I traded urban living for the remote Chiricahuas. What genetic memories do we share?

The mounds are a triad of conjoined hills that rise about five hundred gentle feet above the stone cabin on forty acres that are no longer mine. I used to watch the sun cross the mounds from my kitchen window; late afternoon shadows caressed their rounded tops and washed the golden glow from the grasses that made the mounds look deceptively soft. Since I left Sulphur Canyon, the mounds are what I have missed the most. In the almost ten years that I have been returning for visits, the mounds, in their persistence, have demonstrated their strength.

When I come back to the Chiricahuas, the steady affirmation of granite and limestone contrasts with the increasing fragility I detect in the plants and animals still inhabiting these mountains. Is life here growing unbearable? Will drought and rising temperatures prove unsustainable to all living things? The brittleness reflected in my past choices is replaced with the resilience of this canyon each time I return. I accept what the mountains offer. I implore the canyon to forgive me for abandoning it.

I spin in a lazy circle, arms straight out from my sides, palms up to catch whatever gifts the canyons might grant. I have only gratitude to offer in exchange, which I present to a late-summer sky clotted with monsoon clouds. I watch the clouds grow ripe with the promise of more rain, bringing hope to a desert in drought. Clouds presage rain;

clouds can also portend gloom. Pressed between the clouds, sunlight streams into my palms before fat raindrops seep, then evaporate.

At this elevation, just shy of five thousand feet, I have a wide-angle view of this region and within it, a microcosm of its history. The San Simon Valley stretches between two sister ranges: on the east side, in New Mexico, the Peloncillo Mountains silhouette the sunrise like a two-dimensional cutout of a landscape, and on the west, on the Arizona side, the muscular Chiricahua Mountains, twenty miles wide, are deep enough to swallow the sun. I drop into their silence and listen for the heartbeat messages the two sisters broadcast across the valley, eavesdropping on the conversations they have been having for eons. I've heard it said that mountains speak when they're spoken to. I know otherwise. Mountains speak when they're listened to.

These mountains buzz with the murmurs of past inhabitants of this valley. I want to understand the stories of those who came before me in order to give context to my own history. Stories of homesteaders, ranchers, and miners in nascent territories, spurred west by an expanding economy. Cochise, Juh, Lozen, and the other Chiricahua Apaches who belong to these mountains as much as the mountains belong to them. The European explorers blind to the inhabitants of the area, claiming land in the name of king and destiny. The tribes of the Pueblos, a Spanish word that means both "villages" and "people," an indication of how closely the people are allied with the place they inhabit. And all those who lived here before them, stretching back tens of thousands of years. The stories of these ancestors reverberate like mountain thunder and remind me that I'm new here.

I had moved to the Chiricahua Mountains on a whim, not expecting to stay. When I moved from this place, I doubted I would ever come back, but I have found and invented reasons to return. Each time I visit, I am amazed anew that the sunrise still paints the Chiricahuas with an early morning glow and the canyons still throw the same shadows. The mountains haven't changed, at least not as far as I can tell; it's my perspective that has shifted.

The ancient Irish believed that heaven and earth exist in closest proximity in the thin places. The landscape of thin places is alive with the visible and the invisible, so intimate they share the same frequency. The ancient Irish felt that in a thin place, there is time and space for eternal things like splendor and love. They recognized that in a thin place, where the veil between the sublime and the profane is insignificant, mystery marries nature in a passionate embrace. A thin place calls your attention to these things if you're listening. The more closely you listen, the more you learn, the more you love. You can choose how you want to love and for how long. If you choose to love a constellation or a mountain, you can love it forever.

In a thin place, you can glimpse what connects you to another living thing—a sycamore tree, a golden eagle, a mountain, a person. And yet you can never know the other completely—the mystery remains. Other ways of knowing become possible. It is said that if you embrace the unknown of a thin place, your heart will open and be filled with joy, leaving no room for pain and doubt.

The air drifting to the top of the mounds smells of the rain that rattled the desert floor just an hour earlier. The storm rolls away as the last lightning stabs at the Peloncillo Mountains across the valley. A powerful breeze plays with my hair. I sense that in the decade since I quit Sulphur Canyon, what I have lost has intensified. I am missing the kind of intimate connection with a place that goes so far back it becomes history. My great-grandparents must have felt that kind of bond with their townlands in County Kerry, Ireland. Although farmers in Ireland in the 1800s were tenants not allowed to own the land they worked, they were deeply committed to the place where they lived. Their attachment was based on economics and tradition reaching back through generations, rooting them in such a way that leaving became a ridiculous notion. But circumstances have a way of forcing change.

My paternal grandparents left Kerry in 1892, each in their own time, but they eventually found each other and made a new life together in Chicago. They arrived during the city's transformation from the wetlands home of the Council of the Three Fires—the Ojibwe, Odawa, and Potawatomi Nations—to a major metropolis. The city became a new kind of home, where they raised a family with new dreams of belonging.

The leaving doesn't have to be harder than the staying. I knock on a branch of a narrow creosote bush as I say this. The ancient Irish believed that a genius loci, a guardian spirit, lived in every mountain, mound, wash, tree, and stone. Touching a tree in deference to its spirit, out of respect and gratitude, keeps the gods on your side. Before the paganism of the ancient Irish was subsumed by Christianity, nature was the language of the gods.

The ancient Irish carved one of the first recorded alphabets on granite ogham stones that rise like signposts in farmers' fields and pastures. These stones still stand throughout County Kerry, some not far from my grandparents' townlands. Each letter in the ogham alphabet represents a different tree. Most of the inscriptions on these standing stones can be translated into the name of the local landowner, who more than a thousand years ago claimed the fields and grasses and mountains as belongings, as if carving his name in stone could grant permanence.

The first ogham stone I saw was outside of Cahersiveen, a town built on the slopes of Bentee, a hill whose name in Irish, *Binn an Tí*, means "peak of the house." I was amazed to find the slender free-standing monolith in a grassy field, rising as high as my shoulder, unprotected from both the weather and the flock of sheep that grazed at its base. The slash markings on the edge of the stone were weathered and difficult to read; I could only recognize a handful of letters. In the ogham alphabet, my name begins with the letter *Ruis*, which is associated with the elder tree. The Irish name for this tree is *trom*, or the tree that bears heavy weight.

I had been traveling the narrow Kerry roads looking for ghosts. My search brought me to my grandfather's village at the foot of Cnoc na dTobar ("Hill of Wells," spelled "Knocknadobar" in English). The summit was a site for pre-Christian Lúghnasa festivals, a ritual that kept alive the passion of local folks for the land and its history. Farmers celebrated the beginning of the August harvest by carrying flowers to a peak overlooking the landscape and then burying them as an offering. The trail to the summit of Cnoc na dTobar is now marked with the stations of the cross, which tourists can walk as part of the Pilgrim Paths.

I didn't hike the 2300-foot trail; my faith in Catholic traditions disintegrated long ago, before I left Chicago as a teenager. But at the base of the mountain I felt a surprising sense of belonging, a belief that I was defined in this moment through my conscious observation of it. The knowledge that my father's father, who was dead before I was born, had been a sheep farmer on this green patch of earth with a view of Dingle Bay grounded me here with a connection that startled me.

My grandmother Maggie O'Connell came from a village a few miles inland from Cnoc na dTobar, in a verdant valley far from the tour buses that this morning had clogged the Ring of Kerry. I drove down country roads that grew increasingly narrow and sinuous. Sheep branded with blue and purple paint roamed fields in shades of iconic Irish emerald; kids' swing sets stood in yards adjoining well-kept white-painted houses. The mountains of the Glenbeigh Horseshoe formed a dramatic backdrop to my destination. I was falling under the spell of a romanticized Ireland.

And then I saw the ruins of the Bahags workhouse. After centuries of British rule, English "guardians" forced their Irish tenant farmers into workhouses during *An Gorta Mór*. In 1845, the Bahags workhouse housed a fever hospital on the top floor, staff rooms on the middle floor, and quarters on the ground floor for 400 "inmates," whose numbers swelled to 1,240 at the height of the famine. For some minutes I stood staring at the roofless three-story shell of stone and shadow that reverberated with the despair of those who had lost so much. Eventually I mustered the courage to approach the entrance, where a shallow circle inscribed in a square of cement held dirty rainwater; a faded sign bolted to a rusted metal gate read, "Disinfectant: Dip your boots." I passed under archways and along crumbling walls that held thousands of secrets. Wooden bars still blocked the glassless windows on the ground floor, although the desperate would have had no reason to escape and the dying would have had little strength to even try. Green vines climbed walls in search of sunlight; scrawny grasses poked through stone windowsills. Flocks of rooks and crows circled erratically overhead, screaming angrily as I stood in the center of the void, trembling with an inescapable chill.

There is a gap in my family's history in the years before and during *An Gorta Mór*, when the Irish died faster than the English cared to count. Time and what's knowable got jumbled during the Hunger Years, when records were either destroyed or deliberately not kept. I don't know how my grandmother's family in the countryside managed without the fresh seafood that sustained my grandfather's family along the rocky coast. I do know that Maggie's parents were toddlers during the worst of *An Gorta Mór*, enduring the years between 1849 and 1854 when 50,000 families were evicted from their tenant farms. Her family was fortunate enough to survive starvation, typhus, and dysentery— not an easy task in a ravaged country.

About a mile from the Bahags workhouse is the Srugrena burial grounds, where a local Kerry farmer held the contract to dig graves for the countless bodies that were hauled out of the fever hospital, a tiny fraction of the one million Irish people who died during the Hunger Years. Small rough-hewn stones scattered across the grasses mark the resting places of the nameless dead. A slab of granite stands inside the cemetery gate. Its Irish inscription translates to "Pray for all us souls who died in the Great Famine and are buried in this graveyard."

A few of the graves at Srugrena have headstones. A legend at the entrance led me to the final resting place of Maggie's parents, my great-grandparents Michael O'Connell and Catherine Sheehan. The dates on the headstone show that they both died in 1891, forty-five years after the worst of *An Gorta Mór*. I don't know exactly when they were born, but I do know that neither one reached their fiftieth birthday. I found my ghosts in Srugrena, *Sruth Gréine* in Irish, or "Stream of the Sun."

I bend my knees and sit on the ground on a Sulphur Canyon mound, careful to avoid creosote twigs and cholla spines. The dirt is hard-packed; tiny pebbles press into the backs of my legs. My genius loci is alive on this mound. It vibrates under me with the heartbeat of all the ghosts whose paths I have crossed. A breath of wind carries their names—Chiricahua names, American names, Irish names. When I say my grandmother's name out loud, the wind whisks the sound of my voice off the top of the mound and into the valley. I listen for an echo but hear none.

Maggie's name begins with *Muin*, the letter in the ogham alphabet linked with blackberry, the fruit of the bramble bush. Like the elderberry, it is associated with a time of great fruitfulness. Blackberry brambles grow by sending out runners that root where they reconnect with the earth and create something new.

Maggie was twenty-three years old—past the age most women married in late nineteenth century Ireland—when she booked passage on a steamship to Ellis Island in 1892 after her parents died. It's unclear from the ship's manifest if she traveled alone or with one of her five sisters. She carried expectations and little else other than more determination than fear. What courage did she summon to gamble everything on the unknown? What regrets did she leave behind? I see my grandmother boarding that ship, her long dark hair braided down her back, her face turned toward the sun. I imagine her future awaiting her like an open invitation. How did she contain the heartbreak of leaving those she loved? Her younger sister Clara, according to the 1901 census, was a school monitor in County Kerry. Her uncle Pelagius was named for a fifth century theologian who believed in free will. Her aunt, for whom I am named, came to the United States and joined the Sisters of Saint Francis of Perpetual Adoration. I picture my Irish family in my imagination, but I don't know how to fit myself into their sense of time.

The Irish pagans took a different approach to time. Beginnings didn't move into endings; the ancient Irish rejected straight-line continuity because it wasn't creative enough to allow for a change of mind, wasn't expansive enough to accommodate receptivity to new ideas. They conceived of time as moving in circles—all around, up and down, rising and dropping to new levels. They thought in images that moved in cycles, like the music of a mountain stream measured with a heartbeat that begins again each season.

I think my grandmother might have liked it here in the Chiricahua Mountains. She might have been surprised by the subtle colors of the desert, so unlike the brilliant greens she was familiar with in Kerry. But I like to believe she would have felt the same connection I feel, that she would have understood the language of the desert and felt its pulse. As I picture her in Sulphur Canyon, the veil between my world and hers grows even more translucent. Her story could have been my story if I had been born just a hundred years earlier.

If I tally up all my grandmother's successes and disappointments, I see that her choices led me here. What was she, a country girl from a remote corner of Ireland, thinking when she arrived in an industrial

American city busily preparing for a world's fair? How did she live among newly built skyscrapers and brick-paved roads that deadened any sound of the land's heartbeat? What did she think of her good luck, meeting a respectable man from Kerry, the man who became my grandfather? After he died, my grandmother moved several times across Chicago's South Side, always renting, never owning. She never returned to Ireland. By breaking her physical connection with home, she set in motion my own search for something I still haven't found. Like Maggie, I have moved multiple times, from Chicago to Phoenix to San Francisco to Houston to Santa Fe, and along the way, to these mountains. I, too, am a tenant, merely borrowing space here for the time that I exist on this earth, aware that my footsteps aren't the first on this land.

The late afternoon breeze turns chilly. I hike down from the mounds and drive the five-mile length of Sulphur Canyon Road, from its dead-end at the wilderness gate to Stateline Road, a dusty, unpaved road that marks the border between New Mexico and Arizona. These two states determine time differently based on their political need to save daylight. Except for the Navajo Nation, all of Arizona is always on Mountain Time. For most of the summer, if I stand on the Arizona side of Stateline Road, it is an hour earlier than if I stand on the New Mexico side. Back when people used the sun as their timekeeper, they determined the time of day by measuring the length and direction of their shadows. I step away from my car at the edge of the road and watch my shadow walk with me, but it keeps the same angle no matter which side of the road I stand on. If I jog back and forth across the road, I can time travel, at least for a summer. The clock on my phone automatically adjusts for time zones but it can't keep up with me. I run, faster than time, trying to turn back the hours to the days when I lived here. I move with the pulse of the mountains. I feel the weight of time and history shaping something solid and alive. Deep in my body the layers press into so many strata, each with its own characteristics, covered by so much new that melds with the old, like the mountains themselves.

How long must we survive in a place before we can say we belong there? How much time passes after we leave a land before it forgets us?

I drive up Stateline Road, looking west into the canyon. The sun is setting on Portal Peak. John O'Donohue is speaking to me from a podcast. "Landscape is an incredible, mystical teacher, and when you begin to tune into its sacred presence, something shifts inside of you." His voice continues in my headphones as I approach Granite Gap. "We have time zones inside ourselves," he says, "that we can slip into, like diving deep under water where everything quiets. If you could slow down enough, you would come into your rhythm, into a different kind of living with its own unique beat. Being present in the landscape invites you to shift dimensions, to invite a transformation that allows you to truly receive time." And that, he says, is the secret of change.

When I turn my attention back to the road, I watch cloudless sulphur butterflies dancing above the road, announcing the coming season. They have begun their migration in response to their own undeniable rhythm; within days, they will be miles south. Shadows begin to cross the highway. The endless cycle of the sun rising behind the Peloncillos to paint the Chiricahuas dawn-gold will continue even without my witness.

Bought and Sold:
A History of Lies and Broken Promises

What a staggering change has taken place here! And in such a short space of time! Cities which now throb with growth were only dots fifteen years ago, swallowed in the vast panorama of mountain and desert. People who had only vaguely heard of such names as Phoenix, Tucson, El Paso fifteen years ago, are now living in these cities in the hundreds of thousands.

1960s Deming Ranchettes sales brochure

When my father died in Chicago on Christmas Day in 1989, he left his Deming Ranchettes to me in his will. Select Western Lands, Inc., a company that endures today in the archived records of the lawsuits filed against it, had subdivided pristine New Mexican desert fifteen miles east of the city of Deming, population eight thousand at the time my parents bought their ranchettes, into a crazy quilt of eighty thousand half-acre lots. Infrastructure—paved roads, water, utilities—was nonexistent. I was the sudden owner of two of those lots.

I have no good explanation for why I didn't visit my ranchettes immediately. I was curious—just not curious enough to make the three-hundred-mile trip from Phoenix, where I was living when my father died, or the eight-hundred-fifty-mile trip from Houston, where I moved ten years later for graduate school. Even when I occasionally drove back and forth between Phoenix and Houston on Interstate 10, which goes right through Deming, I couldn't be bothered to take the exit. I glanced south toward the mountains and imagined my ranchettes somewhere beyond the dust rising from the desert floor, but all I caught were glimpses of a small town stuck in time. I would squint and try to visualize what my father thought he had seen out there, but I saw only the mirage of possibility. And then the moment would pass and I would drive on, until one spring day in 2004 I stopped at the Luna County Courthouse and asked the friendly clerk in the assessor's office for help.

"I'm looking for my father's Deming Ranchettes," I told her. "I'd like to sell them."

"You and everyone else," she said and handed me a new map that was identical to the old map my father had tucked into his files thirty-five years earlier.

> *DON'T BE MISLED BY OUR LOW PRICES—Just as there is need for good family style restaurants as well as the more fancy type of restaurants, so there is need for good honest, unimproved, low-priced property...*
>
> *We wish we could keep this up forever... This is the plain truth. We will not offer any more half-acre Ranchettes when our present inventory is sold.*
>
> Display ad, *Chicago Tribune*, March 3, 1974

I was eighteen years old when my father retired from the Chicago Police Department in 1971. He had raised three daughters on the South Side, teaching us to be as cautious as cops walking the night beat. Now that my two older sisters were married and I was a freshman in college downstate, he could finally be free from the weight of the city and the ordeals of policing. He and my mother looked to the south, to the border states, searching for a welcoming warmth.

My parents had begun scouting properties in Arizona and south Texas in the fall of 1968, cruising with real estate agents down streets lined with newly planted palm trees. They were looking for a life where the static of a scanner, the clang of a jail cell door, and the wail of a squad car's siren would be replaced by the rustle of leaves in an Emery oak or birdsong in a desert willow. Where a breeze carried a hint of hope instead of despair. They longed for a new home away from tiny Chicago lots crowded with two-flats separated only by narrow gangways. The Select Western Lands marketing campaign led them to the broad vistas of the southern New Mexico desert, to an openness they had never felt. In June of 1969 they signed a contract and put ten dollars down on two half-acre Deming Ranchettes. They agreed to pay a total of $598 in ten-dollar monthly installments.

I still have the sales brochure that promised that my parents would "live longer and better in New Mexico," a soon-to-be booming destination. The advertising copy described a bright future that awaited my parents at the base of the Florida Mountains, which my father pronounced—practicing the Spanish he learned from a WGN special—the "florr-EE-duh" mountains. In Spanish, "florida" means "full of flowers," which sounds like a name dreamed up by an creative copywriter who had never seen the monochrome mountains that lurk on the Deming horizon. The mountains had probably been named by a Spanish conquistador roaming the Southwest looking for gold in the mid-1500s. The brochure promoted camping and boating in "the healthiest, sunniest climate in all America," although the closest campgrounds and lakes were more than 60 miles away. A 1960s black-and-white line drawing showed a smiling white everyman dressed in a plaid shirt with rolled up sleeves standing knee-deep in a stream, wearing waders, a fedora, and a fly fisherman's vest, landing a trout, to be deposited in a creel at his waist. "You can rent a boat, and fish and swim, or just laze away a wonderful day (and get back home to Deming Ranchettes in plenty of time for dinner!)" the brochure boasted. To my knowledge, my father never boated, fished, or camped, not even as a boy, although he did once get shot on the job.

I have no time to speak of Chicago's morals, and the less time for that the better for Chicago… Deming's morals are not to be discussed in a newspaper—till she has some.

C.M. Chase, editor of the *Vermont Union*,
traveling from Chicago to Deming in 1882

When it was founded in 1881, Deming's nickname was "New Chicago," an homage of sorts to the city it dreamed of becoming—a vibrant economic hub driven by a railroad. In the 1880s and 1890s, New Mexican ranchers used railcars to ship three thousand head of cattle a day to Chicago; the convergence of railroads in Chicago led the city to become the meatpacking center of the world. The new technology of assembly lines enabled millions of hogs, cattle, and sheep to be butchered and processed every year at packinghouses on the South Side. My grandfather worked at Union Stock Yard for ten years—first herding cattle on horseback, later as a foreman—until his death in 1920. It was not a bad job for an immigrant Irishman.

The odors of the killing floors branded my childhood: a Windy City summer breeze carried the stench of manure, sweat, and terrified animals from their pens to my high school, just a mile away, and through my open bedroom window, less than five miles away. The stockyards supplied the meatpacking industry for more than a hundred years before shipping live animals gave way to transporting beef and pork in refrigerated railroad cars. Before the pens and chutes in the yards were dismantled in the late 1960s, classes of grade school children toured the stockyards to witness firsthand the modernization of food processing as each hog was shackled by its hind leg and lifted live onto a giant wheel that passed it and thousands of others along to the slaughterman. This new technology was a first step among many to separate people from their food, from the land that fed them.

By the mid-1800s, U.S. government and commercial interests were desperate to transport people and their belongings from coast to coast in a way that didn't involve a cramped stagecoach, a wooden seat in a wagon train, or a five-month cargo ship voyage around South America. Their attention turned to railroads, which had already successfully transformed travel and commerce along the East Coast. They believed a railroad that connected the coasts would power the country's western migration and help fulfill its manifest destiny.

On January 6, 1853, U.S. president-elect Franklin Pierce and his wife survived a train wreck that violently killed their only surviving child. Pierce's wife, Jane, never recovered from her grief; Pierce drank heavily. His presidency quickly got tangled up with both slavery and the building of the railroad, issues twisted together as the country expanded westward. In one of his first cabinet appointments, Pierce named Jefferson Davis secretary of war and made him responsible for the future of the railroad—a decision fraught with political and moral complications.

Congress immediately authorized Davis to conduct surveys to "ascertain the most practicable and economical route" for a new transcontinental railroad. In a country so intensely divided over the issue of slavery, politicians couldn't agree on much, including the rail route to connect the coasts. Three routes were under consideration: a northern, a central, and a southern route. Every industrialist and investor had his own reasons for his choice while politicians rushed to buy land along the route they advocated as the best for the country.

Davis, who by the 1850s owned more than a hundred enslaved people on his Mississippi plantation, favored the southern route. A Library of Congress photograph shows Davis and his family twenty years after the end of the Civil War, during which he served as president of the Confederate States. A proud man sits front and center with a toddler on his lap, surrounded by his daughter, wife, and grandchildren. Behind the family in the doorway leading into the house stands an unnamed Black woman in a maid's uniform, her right arm behind her back clasping her left elbow. She stares directly into the camera with a penetrating look of apprehension, disillusionment, and smoldering defiance.

Although Davis publicly argued that a railroad could carry troops to California to defend the newly discovered gold there, he personally believed a southern route would open the West for slavery and help the South compete commercially against the North. The surveys showed that the southern route would be the least expensive if it skirted through passes in the Peloncillo and Chiricahua Mountains south of the border of the New Mexico Territory, across land that still belonged to Mexico. Under the terms of the Treaty of Guadalupe Hidalgo, which ended the Mexican-American War in 1848, Mexico had already ceded land north of the border that would become seven U.S. states. But one of the few things U.S. politicians did agree on was that they wanted more. Pierce appointed Davis's friend and fellow Southerner James Gadsden as U.S. minister to Mexico to negotiate moving the international border even farther south.

Gadsden had been the president of a railroad in South Carolina from 1840 until 1850 and, like Davis, favored the southern route to California, where he planned a plantation supported by slave labor. Also like Davis, Gadsden was a slave owner; a year after his death in 1858, his estate auctioned off 235 enslaved people, ranging from infants to seniors, to fourteen bidders in Charleston. He had intended to use slave labor to build the railroad.

Gadsden traveled to Mexico City in 1853 to negotiate with Mexican President Antonio López de Santa Anna. Santa Anna thought Gadsden was an arrogant jerk; Gadsden believed Santa Anna was an incompetent narcissist. Both were probably right. Largely because he needed the money, Santa Anna ultimately accepted $10 million for the thirty-thousand-square-mile Mesilla Valley—a fertile flood plain west of El Paso that included the area that would become Deming.

After the purchase moved the border, locals realized that remaining where they were meant they would have to become U.S. citizens; to maintain their status as Mexicans, they had to move south. Some landowners had inherited their property via land grants, title to which was considered irrevocable. The governments first of Spain and then of Mexico had granted large tracts of land to anyone who would settle them. Land was granted to individuals as well as to entire communities, who shared common spaces for grazing, hunting, and water rights. By 1850, more than 280 land grants covered 15 million acres in New Mexico Territory.

The Treaty of Guadalupe Hidalgo guaranteed protection of all property rights for Mexican citizens living in the New Mexico Territory, including land grants. But a 2004 report from the U.S. General Accounting Office admits: "Whether the United States has fulfilled its obligations under the 1848 Treaty of Guadalupe Hidalgo, with respect to property rights held by traditional communities in New Mexico, has been a source of continuing controversy for over a century.... The effect of this alleged failure to implement the treaty properly, heirs contend, is that the United States either inappropriately acquired millions of acres of land for the public domain or else confirmed acreage to the wrong parties."

Open land not deeded through a land grant could be claimed through squatting rights. Spanish and Mexican custom allowed "unused" land—a description that completely ignored evidence of a recognizable lifestyle among Native people who hunted pronghorn and mule deer on a landscape that doubled as defense—to be claimed. Squatters, in turn, often sold land to speculators for huge profits, if they weren't run off first. Some settlers naïve to the burgeoning corruption in territories where laws were still being written bought phony deeds from the Santa Fe Ring, a group of lawyers and speculators who sold land they didn't own and then foreclosed on the properties when the buyers missed their payments. By 1885, the Santa Fe Land Office was exposed approving fraudulent property claims; the surveyor general of the New Mexico Territory called the deals "systematic robbery" and "the wholesale plunder of the public domain." Territorial Governor Edmund Ross determined that the problem was so serious he recommended the repeal of all laws for the disposal of public lands in New Mexico.

It was through this patchwork of rights that the country was planning a railroad. Congress had agreed on a route only after the Southern states, whose lawmakers opposed the central route, seceded from the Union. Although faced with the staggering costs of the Civil War, President Abraham Lincoln, a former railroad lawyer, signed the Pacific Railway Act of 1862, authorizing the construction of the first transcontinental railroad along the central route. Work began in 1863 and took six painful years to complete. Over time, the federal government granted 91.2 million acres of "public land" to an expanding network of large and small railroad companies; Western states granted an additional 37.8 million acres.

Not everyone welcomed the change agents carving up the landscape, especially locals who owned ranchos on the half-million-acre Las Vegas Land Grant in northern New Mexico Territory. New Mexican homesteaders and cattle ranchers new to the area and unsympathetic to the concept of common-use property started to erect fences in the late 1870s to keep their livestock in and all others out. Las Gorras Blancas ("The White Caps") formed a vigilante group in response to what they considered an attack on their traditional way of life. They recognized how differently they valued land—for its usefulness for farming and grazing—from the newcomers' view of land as commodity. Land grant owners viewed their property as the inheritance they would pass down to future generations; the new Americans saw the large expanses of land in New Mexico as an easy way to accumulate wealth. From 1889 to 1891, these hooded night riders surreptitiously cut fences and burned railroad bridges. They coerced Spanish-speaking New Mexicans to stand with them against the wealthy and powerful Anglo newcomers.

Las Gorras Blancas had the support of their community, and at their peak their numbers swelled to an estimated three thousand. A member of Las Gorras Blancas who had been elected to the New Mexico Territorial Legislature said in a speech to the House of Representatives in February 1891, "Gentlemen, I have served several years' time in the penitentiary, but only sixty days in the legislature...I have watched the proceedings here carefully. I would like to say that the time I spent in the penitentiary was more enjoyable than the time I have spent here. There is more honesty in the halls of the Territorial prison than in the halls of the legislature. I would prefer another term in prison than another election to the House."

> *A citizen, simply as a citizen, commits an impertinence when he questions the right of any corporation to capitalize its properties at any sum whatever... Land has been given to these railways... The land was at the time almost worthless, and but for these railways would have remained so during a long period.*
>
> "The West and the Railroads," Sidney Dillon,
> President of the Union Pacific Railway Company,
> April 1891

By the time my parents discovered Deming in 1969, marketeers were promoting the city as the historic site where the Southern Pacific Railroad met the Atchison, Topeka and Santa Fe Railway. By 1965, Interstate 10 had replaced an older highway system through southern New Mexico, putting Deming on cartoon maps that graced placemats in Howard Johnson restaurants from coast to coast.

Deming was named after Mary Ann Deming Crocker, wife of Charles Crocker, one of the railroad industry's "Big Four" executives.

Little is known about Mary Ann, a Gilded Age woman with a pile of white curls, other than her philanthropy in San Francisco. She never visited the city that bears her name; she never stepped onto the planked platform at the train depot or paused in front of the Santo Niño Chapel, an adobe church with a lopsided bell tower.

I have traveled the streets of Deming, down wide, paved streets named Zinc and Lead and Tin, under the overpasses that carry the railroad tracks over Gold Avenue. I've seen the memorial that commemorates the site of that adobe church, the first Catholic church in Deming, now long gone. I have walked past the building on the corner of Pine and Silver that was the home of the first bank in Deming. Its once-red bricks are now painted beige; the second-story window arches and keystones are painted white. An antiques store occupies the second floor, and the Italian restaurant on the main floor offers a Sunday buffet for $10.95. I've tried to picture my parents enjoying this buffet, after driving up Pine Street from the Butterfield Stage Motel, named for the Wells Fargo stagecoaches that operated for the Butterfield Overland Mail Company. I've imagined them discussing, over meatloaf and mashed potatoes, their frustration at the delays and red tape stopping them from building on their lots. I wondered when they began to realize their dream would not come true. I've wondered if Mary Ann Crocker dreamed of Deming, or if she thought about the city at all.

Records are sketchy, but her New Yorker husband probably came to Deming only once. After capitalizing on the gold rush in Sacramento, Charles Crocker started his railroading career as an investor and got on board by managing the construction of the Central Pacific from California to Utah. It was Crocker's idea to bring thousands of Chinese farmers to replace the few hundred Irish laborers laying track. The Irish had emigrated to Boston to escape the Great Hunger of 1845 to 1849; men looking for jobs were shipped west to work for the Union Pacific, the rival rail line that ultimately met the Central Pacific at Promontory

Point, Utah in 1869. After striking for more pay and better working conditions, the Irish workers were replaced by Cantonese immigrants who were fleeing a bloody civil war. The Cantonese men did the dangerous work of blasting tunnels through granite, cutting grade, and laying track through deep snow. Under pressure from the ruthless construction foreman James Harvey Strobridge, crews got the job done seven years ahead of the government's deadline, winning huge bonuses for the company. Hundreds of Chinese workers died in the process.

The Big Four gained control of the Southern Pacific Railroad in 1868, three years after the end of the Civil War. The southern halves of what would become the states of Arizona and New Mexico had joined the Confederacy in 1861, partly because the residents were convinced the U.S. Army was not doing enough to protect them from the Apaches. The four bands of the Chiricahua Apaches had been resisting encroachment on their land from both American and Mexican settlers. The Apaches believed that land was a living thing, part of all life, a gift from the Creator. It was not something that could be owned and therefore, it could not be stolen.

[Indian removal] will separate the Indians from immediate contact with settlements of whites; free them from the power of the States; enable them to pursue happiness in their own way and under their own rude institutions; will retard the progress of decay, which is lessening their numbers, and perhaps cause them gradually, under the protection of the Government and through the influence of good counsels, to cast off their savage habits and become an interesting, civilized, and Christian community.

"On Indian Removal," President Andrew Jackson,
Message to Congress, December 6, 1830

The history of conflict between the Chiricahua Apaches and the U.S. military is part of the long history of the struggle among the inhabitants of Mexico, New Mexico, and Arizona. A good place to begin to unravel the record is with Cochise, a leader of the Chokonen band of Chiricahua Apaches, and George Bascom, a young, inexperienced Army lieutenant barely three years out of West Point. In 1861, Bascom accused Cochise of kidnapping a settler's twelve-year-old stepson. Cochise insisted he had nothing to do with the boy's disappearance but offered to help find him, believing that he had been taken by another band of Apaches. Bascom accused Cochise of lying; Cochise thought Bascom was joking. When Bascom arrested Cochise, his wife, his two children, his brother, and two nephews, Cochise escaped by slicing through the canvas tent where they were detained. Bascom held Cochise's family hostage; in turn, Cochise took American hostages. Accounts of what happened next disagree. Some say Cochise killed his hostages first and that in retaliation, one of Bascom's men hanged Cochise's brother and nephews. Other versions say that Cochise's brother and nephews were killed first and left hanging for days or weeks at Apache Pass until Cochise found their bodies. I trust a more nuanced view of cause and effect—I don't think either side fully comprehended the scope and the gravity of the war they were engaged in— although the odds were clearly stacked against Cochise.

Seeking revenge for the murder of his family, Cochise called on all four bands of Chiricahua Apaches—Chokonen, Bidanku, Chihende, and Ndendai—to join the fight against the incursion of the settlers, miners, and military into Chiricahua land. His father-in-law, Mangas Coloradas (Dasoda-hae), fought with Cochise for two years, but by 1863, he was more than seventy years old and ready for peace. He agreed to meet James Henry Carleton, an Army general with a categorical hatred of Apaches, under the white flag of peace. Mangas Coloradas was tricked, captured, tortured, and murdered; his body was mutilated. His killing intensified the war between the Chiricahua Apaches and the

American military. As the Apache Wars continued, Cochise believed he was winning as he saw forts being abandoned and fewer white settlers remaining. He was unaware that the Civil War was drawing the U.S. military, and consequently settlers, back east.

In 1869 Cochise told Captain Frank Perry, "I have not one hundred Indians now. Ten years ago I had one thousand." The Civil War had been over for four years, and army troops were returning to the territory. Cochise was beginning to realize that peace would be necessary for the survival of his people. In October 1872, in his sixties and suffering from what was probably cancer, Cochise met with General Oliver Howard and agreed to a settlement, saying, "No one wants peace more than I do." Cochise asked for and was given food, supplies, and a homeland for his people that included the San Simon and Sulphur Springs Valleys from north of the Chiricahua Mountains to the Sonoran border between the Peloncillo Mountains and Dragoon Springs, a total of about fifty-five square miles.

Cochise remained on good terms with General Howard and Fred Hughes, the clerk at the new Chiricahua reservation, who described Cochise as a tall, handsome man of integrity. Upon meeting him, Hughes wrote, "[He] took me by the hand with both of his, told me he had heard of me before and that from this day on he was going to be my friend. He kept his word till the day of his death." The U.S. Army, however, did not. The Chiricahua Indian Reservation was closed upon executive order and the lands "restored to the public domain." This retraction of the agreement negotiated by Cochise split the Chokonen. Led by Cochise's older son, Taza, fewer than half agreed to be relocated to the San Carlos Reservation, which had been established by President Ulysses S. Grant in 1872, about a hundred miles to the north. One Chiricahua Apache called the San Carlos Reservation "the worst place in all the great territory stolen from the Apaches." Cochise's younger son, Naiche, and Geronimo fought side by side before Cochise's surrender; they avoided disease and starvation at San Carlos by escaping with their families to Mexico, where they renewed their fight against the Americans.

Geronimo was a Chiricahua Apache from the Bidanku band. Mexican troops had killed his mother, wife, and three young children during a raid in 1858. The first battle Geronimo led was an act of revenge. He had been told in a vision that weapons would never kill him, and in his later years validated the prophecy by lifting his shirt to reveal bullet holes in his torso big enough to hold small pebbles. Geronimo expanded his fight for retribution against Americans and Mexicans until he and his warriors surrendered to General George Crook in March of 1886 in the Sierra Madres. But when a liquor dealer with an interest in prolonging the Apache Wars told the prisoners that the army intended to murder them when they crossed the border into the U.S., they escaped back into Mexico.

Crook was immediately replaced by General Nelson Miles, who viewed Crook's failure as a challenge. He deployed hundreds of soldiers, dozens of Apache and Navajo scouts, and hundreds of civilians to hunt down Geronimo and his exhausted band. At dawn on September 4, 1886, Geronimo, Naiche, and about three dozen other Chiricahua Apaches formally surrendered in Skeleton Canyon in the southern Peloncillo Mountains to Miles after traveling from Mexico escorted by Lieutenant Charles Gatewood. Geronimo's understanding of the terms of surrender was that all Chiricahua Apaches, some of whom were being held prisoner at Fort Bowie, Arizona, would be reunited within two years. He understood that was the promise made to the Chiricahua people. Like all Apaches, Geronimo expected his children to live on the land of his ancestors. Miles, however, put nothing in writing. Soldiers loaded the prisoners, including Naiche, Geronimo, their families, and dozens of Native scouts who had served the army, onto Southern Pacific prison cars at Fort Bowie. The six-day haul carried them through Deming to Fort Marion, Florida, a seventeenth-century Spanish fortress stinking of rot and disease.

There, officers separated forty-four Apaches ages twelve to twenty-two from their families and sent them to the Carlisle Indian Industrial School in Pennsylvania. The government moved three hundred surviving members of Geronimo's band several more times before locating the prisoners of war at Fort Sill in Oklahoma Territory in 1894 and promising them land if the fort were ever decommissioned.

Geronimo was around eighty years old in 1909 when he fell from his horse after a night of heavy drinking. He caught pneumonia and died at Fort Sill. After Geronimo's death, the War Department released the Chiricahua Apaches from their prisoner-of-war status. After twenty-eight years as prisoners, one hundred sixty-three people moved—in an event known to the Apache people as the "Parting"—to the Mescalero Apache Reservation to join a people they barely knew and to whom they were only distantly related. Seventy-eight chose to stay near Fort Sill on scattered allotments of land that had once belonged to members of the Kiowa and Comanche tribes who had died.

The injustice that shaped the West haunts the unmarked graves and burial places of the people—Apache and military, rancher and farmer, settler and miner—who lost their lives here. I know that some voices have been lost on winds that carry a palpable sense of grief. I do not know all of the truths of the past; I only know some of the stories passed down through generations, told around campfires and corrals, written in letters and in ledger books, that have survived.

The Chiricahua Apaches keep their stories within their families; the histories available to non-Apaches like me are repeated over the years through channels with a point to prove, a perceived wrong to right, a reputation to uphold. In a gift to the historical record, S.M. Barrett, a white man in Oklahoma, received permission to record Geronimo's story, saying, "I wrote to President Roosevelt that here was an old

Indian who had been held a prisoner of war for twenty years and had never been given a chance to tell his side of the story, and asked that Geronimo be granted permission to tell for publication, in his own way, the story of his life." Some of Geronimo's descendants also grew to trust a white woman named Eve Ball who lived near the Mescalero Apache Reservation. For more than twenty years she recorded the stories of the sons and daughters of the Chiricahua warriors and leaders. These generations of stories paint a larger picture; they combine to form a culture of memories.

I was never a good history student—not in grade school, high school, or college. History felt so dry to me, drier than the desert, and older, too. But owning a piece of land made me want to learn its story, and in doing so, I now know about the people before me who believed that land could not be bought or sold, that it was a gift to be cared for and grateful for, and others who wanted to own land at all costs, including deception, theft, and murder. History is not a compendium of facts about things that happened. History is alive with change as new truths are uncovered, as new voices are heard and new stories are told. I struggle to listen, knowing that our stories today create the new histories of tomorrow.

My family does not share a memory culture; our links to the past were broken on ships that carried Irish emigrants far from a colonizer that had no more use for them. My grandparents met an alien landscape in the streets of Chicago after arriving from County Kerry in 1892. Their footsteps mingled with those of the millions of immigrants who preceded them. A *seanchaí*, a traditional Irish storyteller, keeps history alive by reciting entertaining tales tinged with sadness and longing. But my family descended from the quiet Irish; they told no stories. Instead, they hid the shame of *An Gorta Mór*, the Great Hunger, behind cupped hands, the way my grandmother covered her mouth when she occasionally laughed, unwilling to show too much mirth.

*Do you know people who wake up to sunshine 355 days out of each year… people who don't know what it is to be oppressed by humid heat in the summer or the cold clutch of winter damp? Do you know people who can say that in their State the rate of cancer and heart disease is **half** of what the Nation as a whole faces? Do you know people to whom a suntan is a year 'round commonplace, who work and play in a climate called America's healthiest? We know such people. They live in New Mexico.*

1960s Deming Ranchettes sales brochure

My father's fellow policemen threw a party for him at the station house on his last day on the force. His single-layer retirement cake sported pine trees made of dark green icing on a white buttercream field. It was as flat as the ranchettes and tasted like the refrigerator case at the Jewel. If the pastry chef had ever been to Deming, the cake would have been even drier, the frosting grittier. I'm certain no one at the bakery knew how to spin sugar into tumbleweed.

Retirement turned out to be not as sweet as my father had expected. Deming's boom lasted only a century; the U.S. Army closed a training camp there at the end of World War II and passenger train travel dwindled and died. A third of the population, which has increased by only six thousand in the last fifty years, currently lives in poverty. The U.S. Border Patrol is now the largest employer.

My parents never did build their dream house in the shadow of the Florida Mountains. They kept title to the land only because, like thousands of others who had also been deceived into buying a dream that was merely a mirage, they couldn't sell their tiny piece of desert. Undeterred, they doubled down and, in late 1970, subleased land in a planned new community in Cochiti, New Mexico, on the Pueblo de Cochiti, almost three hundred miles north of Deming.

Although pueblo families have lived on their land for hundreds of generations, the nineteen New Mexico pueblos trace their ability to officially claim their homeland to the Treaty of Guadalupe Hidalgo. Legal disputes continued beyond the U.S. Supreme Court decision in 1913 that control of pueblo lands belonged to the federal government, well into the 1920s, a decade after New Mexico became a state.

The federal government had been planning since the 1930s to construct a dam on the Rio Grande on land belonging to Cochiti Pueblo. As they pushed their plan forward, they threatened to condemn both Cochiti and Santo Domingo Pueblos under the authority of the Flood Control Act of 1960 and relocate everyone who lived there, a total of about three thousand people from both pueblos. Cochiti elders resisted construction of the dam and reservoir until political and legal pressure proved overwhelming. The federal government bulldozed the farms and orchards along the river; pueblo residents lost their homes on the river and moved closer to the central plaza. The U.S. Army Corps of Engineers began construction of the dam in 1965 and filled the reservoir with water ten years later.

In the decade between the authorization of the dam and its completion, a development plan grew to include a residential/ recreational community on half of what remained after the reservoir consumed most of the available agricultural land and seepage from the reservoir flooded the rest. In 1969 the pueblo signed a ninety-nine-year lease with a California developer for the creation of the 6500-acre town of Cochiti Lake with lots to be subdivided and subleased to forty thousand non-Cochiti people. Regis Pecos, former Cochiti Pueblo governor, wrote in 2006 that the proposed community offered "all the amenities of a 'seven-day weekend.'"... In this case the people of Cochiti Pueblo had very little to no experience with a proposed development of that magnitude. It became in time 'the best, worst example of economic development.' It would be a form of genocide led by our people."

In the end, after the Pueblo of Cochiti sued the developer and the developer declared bankruptcy, my parents were released from their ninety-nine-year sublease. But the entire experience was "one of the most tragic episodes in recent history for the people of Cochiti," Pecos wrote. "This was not supposed to happen. The Indian Wars were over.... To see the devastation to all of the agricultural land upon which we had walked and had learned the lessons of life from our grandfathers destroyed before our eyes was like the world was coming to an end. And all we could do was watch."

Today, Cochiti Lake exists as a federally controlled recreation area with a visitor center operated by the Army Corps of Engineers. Recreation.gov calls Cochiti Lake a popular fishing spot, although the New Mexico Department of Game & Fish and the New Mexico Department of Health issue advisories against eating fish from the lake owing to the contaminated runoff from canyons around Los Alamos. The area lies entirely within the boundaries of Cochiti Pueblo but is managed independently—one of the first non-Native residential communities on tribally owned land. Some non-Natives did build homes on their leased land; currently almost as many people (about six hundred) live on leaseholds in the Town of Cochiti Lake as there are registered members of Cochiti Pueblo.

I drove through the town recently to see what, if anything, had changed since my parents had been here. I passed randomly placed houses dotting empty streets. The gray earthen dam replaces the horizon with an anonymous wall; the ghost of what was lost is reflected in water distilled by drought.

Eventually, my parents bought a two-bedroom tract home in an Albuquerque subdivision named Paradise Hills, above the Rio Grande. With the first den anyone in my family ever owned and sliding glass doors to a patio, the house was nothing like the place where I grew up, a blonde brick bungalow with a basement and an attic. They lived in Albuquerque until my father developed scleroderma, a disease that turns organs to stone, and my mother was diagnosed with breast cancer. She died first, at age sixty-one. Weeks after my mother died, my father was diagnosed with prostate cancer. He died five years later, at age seventy-six. They did not, despite what the marketing literature had promised, live longer or better in New Mexico.

"Cochise was very proud of making his word good...
Apaches hated liars."

Asa Daklugie, son of Juh, leader of the
Ndendai band of Chiricahua Apaches

Cochise would have liked my father, who was, in my opinion, the only honest cop in Chicago in the Sixties, when Yippies refused to play by anyone's rules and angry students rioted in the streets. My father had gone to work for the predominately Catholic Chicago Police Department when he returned from the U.S. Navy after World War II. A framed eight-by-ten photograph of his graduating class from the police academy hangs on my bedroom wall. When I was in grade school, he was promoted to the rank of lieutenant during a ceremony broadcast live on WGN, which I watched sitting on our dining room floor in front of our black-and-white TV. He was passed over for a promotion to captain later in his career, for reasons I never heard discussed in our family. I like to think he was asked to make one compromise too many. He took to heart his vow to serve and protect, although the battles he was fighting grew increasingly unwinnable.

In 1966, Dr. Martin Luther King Jr. marched through Marquette Park on the South Side, just blocks from where I grew up. I was traveling on vacation with my godparents that summer, but my neighbors and classmates were there in the park. Folks I knew shouted epithets and threw bricks and rocks at the marchers; one of the rocks hit but did not seriously injure Dr. King. In the wake of the riots that followed King's assassination two years later, Chicago Mayor Richard J. Daley issued his infamous "shoot to kill" order. Daley was angry that Police Superintendent James B. Conlisk allowed policemen to use their own discretion during the rioting, and so became the first official in the country to call for more aggressive measures. His order authorizing police to "shoot to kill any arsonists...and...to shoot to maim or cripple anyone looting any stores in our city" was recorded at a press conference. Two days later, the mayor denied having said any such thing and blamed the reporters for misrepresenting the truth.

Such was the political climate leading into the Chicago summer of '68. Friends who were old enough to dodge the draft joined anti-war protestors on a muggy August afternoon outside the Democratic National Convention. For reasons I can't recall, I stayed home, either because of an awareness of the potential for violence or despite it. When the debate inside the smoke-filled International Amphitheater turned into fistfights over the country's role in the Vietnam War, the brawl spilled out the doors and up the streets. Thousands of demonstrators, including two of my cousins, had already gathered in Grant Park. Daley was at the height of his political audacity and had prepared for this moment. By the time the two groups met, twelve thousand Chicago policemen, six thousand U.S. Army soldiers, and six thousand National Guardsmen were waiting in the fading light on Michigan Avenue across from the Conrad Hilton Hotel, where candidates and convention delegates were staying. Daley's men attacked with tear gas and nightsticks, crushing everyone in their path, including journalists and anyone who tried to assist the wounded. Uniformed cops in riot helmets dragged bleeding men and women to waiting paddy wagons.

I can picture Hubert Humphrey in his room in a top floor of the hotel, watching the live televised broadcast of the convention, awaiting his official nomination for president of the United States. I see him closing the open window as tear gas rose with the chants of "The whole world is watching" from the street below. I can imagine his incomprehension when the news channel broadcasting the convention live broke into the announcement of the vote results to show a tape of police beating people who were later identified by the Chicago Study Team in a 1968 report to the National Commission on the Causes and Prevention of Violence as "persons who had broken no law, disobeyed no order, made no threat. These included peaceful demonstrators, onlookers, and large numbers of residents who were simply passing through or happened to live in the areas where confrontations were occurring." It was at that moment, some say, that Richard Nixon won the election.

My father returned from work that night sick to his stomach. He sat heavy in his favorite corduroy armchair with a new tiredness tugging at the corners of his mouth; he rubbed one hand over the other, as if scrubbing them clean. From where I sat on the floor at his feet, I caught whiffs of the tear gas that clung to his uniform. My father was a reticent man, even for a quiet Irishman, but not that night. He spoke calmly, almost in a monotone, telling stories about the protestors who had occupied the Hilton, dropping baggies of what he genteelly referred to as "human excrement" on the cops below. His eyes asked, *Why? Why?* although he already knew the answer. But just asking the question changed him fundamentally.

The National Commission on the Causes and Prevention of Violence, formed three months before the convention, ultimately declared the Battle of Michigan Avenue a "police riot." My father had been assigned to the traffic detail in the area that night. Within a year, he bought land in New Mexico, and within three years he retired.

Many "land for sale" offers involve half-acre lots known
as Deming Ranchettes. Thousands of tiny Ranchette

lots were subdivided from the open range many years ago, and some of them are lovely, but to this day most Ranchette lots are vacant and unusable.

"The Code of the West: The Realities of Rural Living, 2013 Edition" published by the Luna County Manager, Deming, New Mexico

After several missteps, I found my two half acres at the corner of Ironwood and Don Fernando Roads, barely discernable scratches in the desert marked only by a weathered stick that had fallen to the ground. The map given to me by the clerk in the assessor's office had directed me down dead-end streets, unpaved roads with limited signage, and faint hints of tire tracks through dried grasses. When I arrived at my lots, I appreciated how primitive undeveloped land could be. There was no electricity, no water, no paved road. Broken glass and tumbleweed littered my land; wind whistled in my ears. I kicked the earth with the toe of my boot, surprised to find a hard-packed crust. The only sign of life was a burrowing owl that regarded me warily.

For almost twenty years after my father's death, I had paid property taxes of five, six, twelve dollars a year to the Luna County Assessor's Office while I tried unsuccessfully to sell my lots. An internet search revealed that Japanese investors were offering Deming Ranchettes for sale for thousands of dollars per half-acre. A crude website created for folks trying to sell their property showed many more listings than sales, and those sales seemed questionable. I researched the recorded owners of lots adjacent to mine and mailed handwritten letters to them asking if they were interested in buying more. No one replied.

But I had overlooked one property owner who was doing his own research and called me in 2007. He said he was my neighbor, although he lived in South Dakota. He quickly got around to asking me if I wanted to sell my Deming Ranchettes.

"The property I purchased is no longer buildable due to the change in Ordinance 37, which Luna County approved last summer," my neighbor said. "It requires a minimum of two acres to drill a well. I have one acre and you have one acre. Neither one of us can do anything without the other."

This was the first time I had heard of this new ordinance, passed in 2006, requiring homeowners to have at least two contiguous acres before they could drill a well. The goal was to isolate wells from a neighbor's septic system, but the effect was to render all single Deming Ranchette lots unbuildable. The information tainted my lots with a new shade of worthlessness.

"Well," I said, "I don't know…"

"The only solution is for property owners to work together on this so it is a win-win situation for everybody. You don't have to give me an answer right away, but let me know what you think. I'll give you my number—you can call me anytime."

Faced with the opportunity to finally sell the property, I was surprised by the strength of my connection to it. Other than his policeman's sweater and nightstick, it was the only possession of my father's that I had. If I could have asked him, my father wouldn't have hesitated to tell me to sell the lots. Like others who believed in the American dream, he assumed that land automatically increased in value over time. I had been raised with the belief, the same one held by the new Americans who acquired New Mexico land 150 years before me, that buying land was accumulating wealth. It was a belief in a dream that was rapidly evaporating.

Select Western Lands addressed all correspondence to my father as "Dear Friend," which should have pinged his cop radar. Would he admit to buying a con man's pretty words? I think my father would acknowledge that he had been overly optimistic, but I'm sure he would stop short of labeling the copywriter a liar and the developer a thief. Sometimes I didn't know what nagged at me the most—the fact that he was swindled or that tricking him was even possible. A religious man, he had so much faith in the promise implied by New Mexico skies that he allowed himself to be fooled. That realization was my biggest loss.

If I had known the extent of land fraud and corruption in New Mexico, I might not have been so surprised. I called my neighbor back, and we struck what we agreed was a fair deal. I sold both lots for $1,000, almost twice what my parents had paid for them forty years earlier. If I subtract the taxes paid over the years, I made about $90 profit, or $2.25 per year. If I add up the decades of a gradually accrued respect for the Arizona/New Mexico borderlands, so far from my childhood on the South Side, I have attained a net gain. My father would be proud.

> We are vanishing from the earth, yet I cannot think we are useless or Usen would not have created us. He created all tribes of men and certainly had a righteous purpose in creating each...
>
> Thus it was in the beginning: the Apaches and their homes each created for the other by Usen himself. When they are taken from these homes they sicken and die. How long will it be until it is said, there are no Apaches?

Geronimo's Story of his Life, Taken Down and
Edited by S.M. Barrett, 1907

Bidanku, Chokonen, Chihende, and Ndendai. Evocative names that trip my Anglo tongue every time. Names that describe and deceive. By some accounts, the name "Apache" is a Zuni word that means "Navajos."

Others believe it is a Yavapai word that means "enemy." Geronimo wrote, "We call ourselves Ndé meaning The People, but to nearly everyone else in the world we were known as The Enemy." Taza, Naiche, Mangas Coloradas, Juh. Geronimo's Apache name was Goyahkla, which some say means "one who yawns." The story that survives suggests that the name "Geronimo" stuck when his Mexican enemies called out in fear to San Jerónimo as they were being attacked on the feast day of St. Jerome. Some translate the name "Cochise" to mean "strong as an oak," which aptly describes the man whose dignified posture and direct demeanor commanded respect from all who met him. "Chiricahua" is most likely what fell from the mouths of Spanish speakers trying to pronounce the indigenous Opata word for "turkey mountain."

In the thirty-five years between my father's purchase of his Deming Ranchettes and the day I stood at the intersection of Ironwood and Don Fernando, many of the descendants of the Chiricahua Apaches who survived the prisons of Florida, Alabama, and Oklahoma reorganized under the name Fort Sill Apache; they became a federally recognized tribe in 1976. Descendants who did not join the Fort Sill Apaches are still fighting for federal recognition as Chiricahua Apaches.

Laws written by white men to govern the status of Native Americans have morphed over decades. Tribes were considered sovereign nations when treaties were signed in the early 1800s, but that sovereign nation status was terminated in 1871. Native Americans were recognized as persons under the terms of the Fourteenth Amendment for the first time in 1879; they were allowed to appeal to the courts in 1881; they were granted full U.S. citizenship in 1924. Various bills were submitted and defeated in Congress to create courts, tribunals, and commissions to resolve, as one analysis put it, "claims involving history and anthropology as much as law." Finally, in 1946, Congress formed the Indian Claims Commission to hear grievances against the government brought by Native American tribes. In its final report, written in 1978 and looking back over its mission, the Indian Claims Commission wrote, "By the

1890s, the contest for America was over and its possession signed, sealed, and delivered. But, though the white man was contented with his record in these dealings, the Indian was not."

One of the first claims decided by the Commission was filed by the survivors of Geronimo's band for unfair imprisonment; the case was dismissed on a technicality. Most petitions asked not for money but for the return of confiscated tribal land. Of the one hundred and eighteen claims filed between 1881 and 1950, only thirty-four tribes were awarded compensation and almost none got their land back. The Fort Sill Apaches filed two lawsuits in 1949—one for land and the other for mineral rights. After twenty-six years of government delays and red tape, the commission awarded the tribe $14 million—one dollar for each of their original fourteen million acres located within U.S. borders.

Two-thirds of that money went to the members of the Mescalero Apache Tribe in New Mexico. Another ten percent paid attorneys' fees. Of the remaining $4.2 million, the Fort Sill Apaches dispersed eighty percent to its members, about $4,800 each. In 1999 the Fort Sill Apaches paid $30,000 to buy thirty acres of creosote and bunchgrass in Akela, New Mexico, nestled between Interstate 10 and the Southern Pacific Railroad tracks. In November 2011 Apache Homelands became the country's newest and smallest Indian reservation, just six miles east of my father's lots.

I drove through Deming recently on the way from New Mexico to Arizona, and stopped at Apache Homelands, a stucco restaurant and smoke shop that sits on a gravel parking lot off a winding I-10 exit. The restaurant is open twenty-four hours, but at lunchtime I saw only two other customers—a pair of uniformed Border Patrol agents balancing trays loaded with soft drinks under a neon Budweiser sign. Fluorescent lights against a low black ceiling lit the dining room, which smelled of fryer fat and spilled beer. Folding tables holding bottles of A1 and Cholula hot sauce crowded a smoky corner. A locked glass case displayed Cuban cigars and cartons of American cigarettes at discount prices. Three abandoned betting windows along a far wall testified to two successive governors' denials of the tribe's requests for gaming. The recirculated air accentuated the feeling that time itself had surrendered.

I passed along two walls that displayed posters narrating the history of the Chiricahua Apaches. In contrast to the versions I had read previously, these stories were told in the voices of Apache elders instead of the white man's uncomprehending and often condescending point of view. Naiche and Geronimo stared out from large sepia-toned photographs, as if still searching for all they had lost.

Unlike the Apaches, my father's immigrant parents wanted to believe that land could be owned, although they themselves never owned any. The Irish had lived more than two hundred years under the Penal Laws, which forbade Catholics from owning or leasing land, serving in the military, or owning a horse worth more than five British pounds. In 1792 Edmund Burke had referred to the Penal Laws as "a machine of wise and elaborate contrivance, as well fitted for the oppression, impoverishment and degradation of a people, and the debasement in them of human nature itself, as ever proceeded from the perverted ingenuity of man." Although my father eventually became a homeowner, his parents and siblings spent part of their lives in apartments, unfamiliar with the joys and the burdens of owning land, knowing all the while that the value of home is not measured in dollars.

Ultimately, my parents' ill health forced them to leave New Mexico and return to Chicago. I never heard them say they were going "home." The city they left had changed in the ten years they were gone—first a white woman and then an African American man had become mayors. The stockyards closed and a Great America theme park opened just north of the city. The tallest building in the world was erected in the Loop. Property values had soared while my parents were in New Mexico; when they returned, they could afford only a third-floor walkup in a south suburb. My sisters, aunts, cousins, nieces, and nephews surrounded them with care in that small condominium, as first my mother and then my father lost their battles against disease.

I turned from the posters of Apache history and approached the cash register, where paper menus in plastic sleeves lay stacked on the counter. I ran my finger down the list of burritos and chicken fried steak and settled on a homemade brownie in a Ziploc baggie. I handed two dollars to a woman wearing a cap embroidered with "Apache Homelands" across the crown. "Sign our guest book?" she asked, pointing to a food-stained log. I added my name and email address under the last entry, made a year earlier. I imagined getting messages from Cochise and Geronimo, telling me their stories. I thanked the woman, headed to the exit, and pushed open the door, squinting hard in the unrelenting light.

How Much Can a Bag Hold?

I was unaware of anything unusual happening out there, a crisis arriving on my doorstep, until my greyhound, who had grown so accustomed to the scores of resident jackrabbits he didn't even notice them anymore, barked. If you spend enough time in the desert where your closest neighbor might be half a mile away, you notice subtle shifts in color, small movements in the mesquite. I had been on the back patio enjoying a breakfast of vanilla yogurt with fresh strawberries and pecans, bought at the Walmart in Douglas, fifty miles south on the Mexican border. I rose from the table at the disturbance and glanced in the direction the dog was barking, but saw only shadows behind the barn, which we used for vehicles rather than horses. The shadows moved when I raised my hand over my eyes to shield the glare.

Two men crouched next to a spigot at the open end of the barn, where a buried PVC pipe carried water from the well. When they saw me walk around to the front of the house, they stood; one waved an empty plastic milk jug over his head. I knew immediately they were not from this valley, which is home to cattle ranchers, retired BLM managers and railroad workers, small business owners, educators, artists and writers, and other folks who defy categorization. I knew why these two guys were there.

The population density in the San Simon Valley was estimated at fewer than twenty people per square mile. At fifty miles north of the U.S./Mexico border between the Chiricahua Mountains in Arizona and the Peloncillo Mountains in New Mexico, I lived at the intersection of the Sonoran and Chihuahuan Deserts—hot and dry during the day, surprisingly chilly at night. It must have been a long and difficult trip for these two men, with few safe places along the way to stop.

When I got closer, I could see that they appeared to be in their late twenties. One wore dusty black pants and a sweatshirt of indeterminate color with a hole in it the size of a bullet. The other was shorter and stockier and wore an adobe-colored T-shirt, faded jeans, and a woolen cap. He had a scar through one eyebrow.

"*¿Tienen agua?*" The one with the scar held the battered milk jug out in front of him, asking for water, too polite to help himself.

"*Sí,*" I said. I kept my eyes on their hands as I reached for their container and leaned over to open the faucet. Like most of the residents in this valley, I grew wary when strangers appeared on my property, although it hadn't always been this way. The one in the sweatshirt shifted his weight from foot to foot and looked nervously over his shoulder. I followed his gaze, searching for Border Patrol vehicles or more migrants. In the desert in the summer, the landscape looks like an overexposed photograph, reflected light bouncing off random objects like naked rock and cholla until the air shines like polished glass. A heat shimmer throbbed above the valley floor. It was only eight o'clock in the morning, but already the temperature was in the nineties.

It was the summer of 2006, the year Border Patrol detained more than one million unauthorized migrants who tried to cross the southern border. How do you count the number of people who cross a political line contrived by governments? How do you tally people who work hard to be invisible? I have seen life-sized shadows duck into washes and behind yucca at the sound of my car approaching on Highway 80. When hiking in Sulphur Draw behind the mounds that rise between the mountains and the house, I came across trash left by people who also hiked these trails, not long before me. At first I was irritated that someone littered *my* hiking trail, practically in *my* backyard. But then I took a closer look at what had been left on the ground—a pair of sneakers so worn through the rubber had come away from the edges of the soles. Empty bottles of pain relievers, labeled "*¡Super fuerte!*"; Band-Aids "*de color piel*"; dented cans of Red Bull. Miniature prayer books. Diapers.

It is more possible—"easier" is not the right word—to count the failures: the border crossers who have died in the desert. Pundits estimate that from 2000 to 2006, an average of 200 migrants died every year crossing the border in Arizona, which was the busiest state in the country for both crossings and deaths. In 2006 Border Patrol rescued more than 2500 migrants from life-threatening circumstances. These statistics do not count those who have never been found. The primary cause of death began to shift in 2005 from exposure—including dehydration, heat stroke, and hyperthermia—to "undetermined," suggesting that human remains were being discovered in more remote areas—in side canyons, deep washes, and rocky ledges—and were more decomposed when found. These statistics challenged me to consider the great hunger that sets a group of people on the move—a hunger for a better life and safety for themselves and their families. The craving for an opportunity, however small, to feel your dreams are not dreamt in vain. Security measured by the incremental removal of negatives, like fewer death threats, less chance of gang violence, reduced degrees of desperation. The too-heavy burden of hope carried by the people who died here.

"*Podemos trabajar*," the one with the scar said. His statement was more than an offer to trade labor for whatever I could give them; it was a declaration of their abilities, an assertion that they were here to contribute. According to estimates from various studies designed to find answers for these dilemmas, 260,000 to 290,000 undocumented migrants worked in Arizona in 2005. An estimated ten to fifteen percent of them harvested the oranges, grapefruit, lemons, tangerines, lettuce, melons, and other fruits and vegetables Arizona is famous for. Many others worked in construction; some did handyman jobs on cattle ranches. Tougher law enforcement, shifting economics, and changing social standards narrowed opportunities for migrants moving north. The two men at my barn were counting on the value of undocumented migrant labor in this new social economy. But on this desert morning, under a sun that made even the cholla appear to perspire, they were hungry men who would be grateful for even half a chance.

Was there any kind of work they could do around the property? I thought of the leaking irrigation lines that ran to the fruit trees and the gate on the trash enclosure that had blown down in the last storm. But I knew we were already being watched.

My neighbor and her husband on the adjacent forty acres to the east had been living at Sulphur Canyon for more than ten years in a mobile home with a yard full of chickens and rabbits. I wouldn't have been surprised if she had already called Border Patrol. More than once she told the story about the two migrants who knocked at her door one evening about three years earlier when her husband had been out of town. When she stepped outside of her double-wide, more than seventy men appeared out of the snakeweed, hungry and terribly thirsty. The neighbor fed them all the food she had, including the beans she had simmered overnight and all the fruit, carrots, tortillas, and pan dulce she had just bought in Douglas. She was afraid that word would get out that hers was a friendly stop along the way north, leading to more of these visits. She was also more than a little worried about what they would do when they learned she had called Border Patrol. She could tell from their lack of swagger they weren't drug runners and therefore were unarmed, but she didn't know what she would do if they started to run away. Would Border Patrol think she had tipped them off? Could she be charged? These were real concerns to anyone living so close to the border, anyone dealing with constantly shifting rules and rumors and judgments. After multiple incidents, she and her husband developed a routine. When migrants appeared on their property, they pulled out a shotgun, commanded everyone to sit down, and demanded they hand over their shoes before calling Border Patrol. "I'm on a pension," she explained to me one afternoon. "I can't afford to feed everyone who comes through here even if I wanted to. Then I would be the one with no food."

Ask a local cattle rancher if he has any stories about hiring the men who traveled through the valley every spring, and he can go back generations. Individuals have been coming through this valley for hundreds of years looking for work. Now ranchers say they can't estimate how many "passers-by" they have fed since they built their homes in this valley. How many meals they shared with strangers with few words in common around the kitchen table. A man passing by would be offered a meal in return for performing a few odd jobs such as mending fences or chopping wood. Like most locals, these ranchers often left their doors unlocked when they weren't home. Migrants would come into their kitchens, help themselves to the leftovers in the ice box, then wash their dishes and leave them turned upside down to dry on the drain board. One rancher told me about coming home to find a note in Spanish listing all the things taken from the house—*pan, queso, agua*—and a few centavos on the table, with an apology. The neighbor to the west, who had worked for the U.S. Forest Service, told me a similar story. "In the old days we used to count on the men coming through to help us with the fencing and fixing. I remember one fella who took off north with my tape measure. He returned it five months later on his way back south. I put him to work that time, too."

No matter which story I repeat, whose version I use, together they form a mosaic that paints basically the same picture. Migrants and locals shared a mutual trust and need for decades until things started to unravel. The Immigration Reform and Control Act of 1986, signed into law by Ronald Reagan, made it illegal to hire the people migrating north from the border. Businesses—including cattle ranches—that knowingly employed unauthorized migrants could be fined up to $2,000 for each person hired. Get caught again and the fines could more than triple. From what I have read, as available migrant jobs in agriculture, construction, and service industries began to decrease, the buyers' market for Mexican marijuana increased. Drug sales became another revenue stream, pursued by people looking for a new way to earn a living. Americans have been buying illegal drugs for decades, and various administrations have funded their own wars on drugs. In my lifetime, that includes Ronald Reagan in 1986 and George W. Bush in 1990, Bill Clinton in 2000, and Mexican president Felipe Calderón in 2006. The same neighbors who used to tell stories about hiring border crossers gradually began telling stories about discovering people hiking over the Chiricahua peaks with pounds of marijuana strapped to their backs. By 2007, the amount of marijuana seized in Arizona had more than tripled in ten years.

"There's so much drugs through here now, you can't trust anybody coming through," my neighbor, the former Forest Service manager, said. "Hell, just last month Border Patrol stopped a hundred and fifty kilos of pot going through Sulphur Canyon. That's just one month—and it's just what they caught."

In the early 2000s, the residents of this valley had increasingly more border crossers showing up unexpectedly on their property. A new sense of danger pervaded the area like a low fog that drapes the foothills and obscures the horizons. At a potluck the evening before my visitors appeared, the conversation, as usual, turned to migrants. Neighbors spoke of houses broken into, things stolen. As we stood beside a buffet table laden with cheese enchiladas, pork tamales, refried beans, and wedding cookies, we shared stories. One woman told of driving home from Douglas along Highway 80, the only paved road coming north from the Mexican border, with a handgun on her dashboard. "I leave it there so they'll see it," she said. Another woman said that one evening, three men who appeared to be migrants stood in the middle of the highway, refusing to move. "Until I gunned it," she said. "There's something intimidating about the sound of my Hummer when I gun it." I didn't ask why she drove a Hummer in a community thirty miles from the closest gas pump, but I did ask what happened next. "They got out of my way and I went on to pick up my kids at school. Whatever you do, don't stop."

The only sounds in the morning stillness were the whirring call of a cactus wren and occasional low clucks from a covey of quail. I knew that aiding undocumented migrants was a felony, punishable by up to five years in prison. In 2006, Border Patrol agents were still on friendly terms with the locals because they were the only law enforcement within a hundred miles. But if the neighbors called Border Patrol (and everyone here had those numbers taped to a kitchen cabinet or stuck on the refrigerator), I could only hope the agents would leave me alone. I knew they would pick up the men at the barn and take them to Lordsburg to begin processing them for deportation. They might also choose to save themselves the paperwork and just drop the men off on the other side of the border near Antelope Wells in a desert area with no facilities for miles, where they would no doubt turn around and cross again. n the summer of 2006 only a five-strand barbed wire fence separated New Mexico from Chihuahua at the crossing at Antelope Wells, the least-trafficked crossing in the country. But in October of that year, President George W. Bush would sign the Secure Fences Act to extend existing border fencing by 700 miles, mostly through Arizona. The Clinton Administration in 1994 and 1995 had built border walls and fences in San Diego, Nogales, and El Paso, and increased the number of Border Patrol agents in those urban areas by a factor of five. Sealing off the well-worn, safer routes of migration shifted traffic to the more rugged parts of the desert. The strategy was to stem the flow of migration into California and Texas; officials assumed that people wouldn't risk their lives crossing through the Arizona desert, including this hot, dry valley. They were wrong. In New Mexico, just five miles from here, that journey is called *La Jornada del Muerto*.

I weighed my options as I handed the filled water jug back to the two men. *"¿De donde vienen?"* I asked. I searched their faces but saw only traces of the formidable obstacles they had met along their journey. The one in the sweatshirt gave me an unexpected half-smile, as if to put me at ease, when it should have been the other way around. I should have been the one smiling, projecting friendliness, but I was still too uneasy. The man with the scar replied that they had come from Agua Prieta, the Mexican town on the border with Douglas that served as a funnel for undocumented migrants. I knew that the border town wasn't where they were from originally. *"¿Pero antes de eso?"* I asked. The one in the sweatshirt said he was from Durango, Mexico; the man with the scar reluctantly admitted he had traveled from Honduras.

"Honduras!" I said, surprised, although I shouldn't have been. *"¿Cuántas semanas que fueron viajar?"* I asked, struggling to remember the present perfect tense of "travel." I had no idea how long a trip from Honduras would take, but I knew it wasn't days. I figured it involved weeks of accepting rides from coyotes, hopping the train called *La Bestia* (also called *el tren de la muerte* and *el tren de los desconocidos*, but always known as the dangerous, illegal, and sometimes only way to get across Mexico), and walking north from Agua Prieta. I tried to imagine preparing for such a long trip. I understood why they would be in my yard holding only an empty plastic milk jug.

"Tres meses," the Honduran said, staring at the ground. He crouched down and picked up a handful of sand, letting it sift through his fingers. *"Es una vida dura,"* he said, so softly I could barely hear him. *"Una vida dura."*

For a second I thought I saw his eyes darken with grief under his woolen cap. I recognized traces of memories crossing his face, no doubt of the past three months, images that haunted him as he wandered: the family he had left—wife, daughters, sons, parents—who waited for his return, for news of where he was and where he would end up. For that brief moment, suspended between his past and his future, now both uncertain, he looked like he had seen a ghost—the ghost of the person he had been when he began this hard journey, a person he scarcely remembered.

Nothing in my history would motivate me to trudge along desert mountain trails at night for three months, but I have never known the kind of misery that drives men and increasingly more women with children to leave behind everything familiar. Border Patrol agents have told me stories about following women's and children's footprints along the edges of steep mountain trails, only to watch the smallest footprints disappear. "We can only assume someone picked up those children and carried them through the narrow spots," the agents said and I hoped they were right. Friends in Portal have told me about watching a line of people filing down a ridgeline at dusk, dressed in traditional Central American clothing that was inadequate protection against the winter snow that was still falling. Poverty, violence, desperation—all strong forces that compel people to weigh fear against risk and begin this journey.

In 1892 my paternal Irish grandparents arrived at Ellis Island, the first dedicated immigrant detention facility in the world. That was forty years after the end of the Great Hunger in Ireland that killed one million people, one-eighth of the population in the country. Six years later, my great-grandfather, a survivor of the Great Hunger, followed my grandparents from the west coast of Ireland to America. From 1800 to 1900 almost four million Irish citizens emigrated to the U.S., including many other members of my family. All crossed borders, hungry for the American dream.

"¿Cuántos kilómetros hasta Willcox?" the Mexican in the sweatshirt asked, pronouncing the name of the town "Weelcoax." "¿Es lejos?"

I wondered what their version of "far" might be and what it would cost them to walk ninety more miles. They could possibly find work in the chile fields around Willcox. A veterinarian there told me that so many undocumented migrants work in those fields that a shantytown called *Perro Flaco*—Skinny Dog—sprang up to support them. Before the drug runners traveled these routes, undocumented migrants thought of the spot as an oasis. Anxious locals considered the place a cesspool filled with drugs and guns. "I'm afraid to drive down that road at night," the veterinarian said. "I'm afraid of what would happen if the car broke down. And I won't stop anymore to help anyone."

Halfway into my explanation about where Willcox sits on the highway, I realized they wouldn't be taking the highway. They listened patiently to my halting Spanish as I changed my thinking from driving ninety miles to walking ninety miles. I tried to picture the twists and turns and detours each part of their trip had already taken, multiplied by the length of their journey still remaining, to whatever city or town they would eventually reach. Not wanting to consider the alternative, I conjured up a happy ending for them somewhere, reunited with their families, finally eating a meal of familiar food.

"*¿Tienen ustedes comida?*" the Mexican in the sweatshirt asked.

I winced, annoyed with myself for not anticipating his question. Clearly they were hungry. "*Sí, claro. Esperen aquí.*" I turned to go back to the house. As I walked, I grew more conscious of the neighbors' watchful eyes. How can it be a crime to give a hungry man some food?

My concern was how little I had to offer them. What could I give them that they could carry across a summer desert? What did I have that didn't need to be cooked or refrigerated or opened with a can opener? I searched for food that wouldn't spoil and for easy-open packages. I found an orange and an apple and a couple of avocados. I stuffed a plastic bag with the fruit and added granola bars, V-8 juice, tortillas, and half a loaf of homemade bread. I carried the bag back to the barn where the two men stood waiting. The bag felt so heavy but seemed to hold so little.

The Honduran took the bag with both hands. "*¡Gracias, gracias!*" they both repeated, dipping their heads and backing away. They held the bag and the water jug close but unopened as they quickly walked north along the base of the mountains. Soon they were out of sight, invisible once again. I never saw migrants on the property again, and for as long as I lived in Sulphur Canyon, to my knowledge, neither did my neighbors.

Many months later, while washing the outside windows of the cabin on a warm day that carried the scent of ozone on a breeze, I thought I caught a brief glimpse of their faces reflected on the surface of the glass. I knew I was imagining it, but their two faces appeared, faintly, under the soap suds and water drips, in patterns that ebbed and flowed, following a course of their own. For a minute as I wiped the glass, their faces stared out at me. Then the water dried and the window cleared.

How Far Would You Go to Save a Rat?

If you live in the desert, you know woodrats. Also known as pack rats, they are the rodents that build nests in the garage and steal the dog's toys from the yard. They especially enjoy dog turds. Greedy little bastards, they'll drop the prize they're carrying to pick up something newer and flashier. I've heard the tale about the pack rat who traded two nickels for a shiny new dime, but I can't tell you if it's true. I can tell you from experience that pack racks will eat the stuffing from your patio cushions and everything in your garden including the jalapeños. They will climb into the air conditioning fan in your car, which you won't discover until miles into a summer road trip to Houston. When the stench and the heat become unbearable you will start praying for a mechanic's shop on an easy exit off the interstate around Van Horn or Ft. Stockton even if you haven't prayed in years.

My problem started small enough—with mice, not rats. Mice are daintier than rats—skinnier tails, more petite feet, less significant droppings—and cuter, too, if you go for big ears and whiskers. At night sitting on cushions scarred by another freshly chewed hole, I heard little mouse rustlings in the flower bed and caught glimpses of quick grey shadows. I sidestepped fresh mouse droppings on walkways and doorsteps. I lifted the lid on the barbeque grill, intending to fire it up and cook a lovely dinner, but stopped cold when I saw a nest filled with a mother mouse and babies blinking back at me, as innocent as puppies.

Not even the great horned owls and barn owls that hunted the property at night could keep up with the rodent proliferation. I often discovered regurgitated owl pellets at the base of the pine trees they roosted in. When I broke the pellets open, I uncovered mouse jaw bones with the teeth still in place, tiny ribs small as parentheses, and breastbones with fur still attached. But even with owls on the prowl, the yard was lousy with mice. Every day for two weeks during that summer's monsoons, yet another mouse, its whiskers fanned out around its head like a crown, floated in the rain barrel that caught precious runoff from the roof. Each morning I would fish the bloated blotch out of the water and the next morning I would do it again.

I considered setting snap traps but was stopped by my fickle boundaries both physical and ethical. The idea seemed suitable on days when my patience wore thinnest. Recent studies have recorded the facial expressions of mice and have correlated these various faces to different emotions, like disgust, empathy, and joy. The cartoonists drawing Mickey and Minnie and Tom and Jerry were on to something. But a mouse's ability to smile and frown doesn't stop researchers from using mice as lab rats.

My property in Sulphur Canyon belonged more to the critters who had been born here than it belonged to me; I measured my history in this valley in years rather than generations. The handful of folks fearless or foolish enough to live in this desert inhabited an environment that outsiders called inhospitable, but the critters called it home. The animals had long ago adapted to a climate with an average monthly rainfall of less than an inch, except during the summer monsoon/flash flood season when three times that much rain falls, sometimes all at once. The humans who relocated here made feeble attempts at acclimation with ceiling fans and evaporative coolers, sunscreen and moisture-wicking fabrics. It was into this ecosystem that I contemplated bringing devices designed to kill. A snap trap would break the neck of anything naïve enough to believe I put that peanut butter there for its enjoyment.

I didn't want to set snap traps, although I can't say that selflessness is my strong suit. It's true that food, shelter, and water are hard to come by in the desert, but whenever resources are in short supply, the laws of the jungle apply. I had no intention of sharing my resources with rodents, but I was willing to cut a deal with the mice. If they stayed out of my house and away from my stuff, I wouldn't kill them. It was that simple. But when I discovered a disheveled mouse nest built of desert litter behind the kitchen counter, I felt violated. My vengeful goal was complete annihilation. With mice, anything less than total truculence gets you nothing but more mice.

Deer mice (*Peromyscus maniculatus*) are the most abundant mammal in North America, a fact I can attest to from personal experience. At the bottom of the vertebrate food chain, they are snacks for coyotes, bobcats, hawks, snakes, and other carnivores I was grateful to have on the property. A female deer mouse can produce up to fifteen babies every two months, and those girl babies can carry on the lineage as soon as they are six weeks old. Captive deer mice have delivered as many as fourteen litters in one year, although three or four litters per year is more typical among wild mice. As a result of a female's fertility and appetite for sex, it is possible to be blessed with a ten-fold population jump every year.

I pulled the bottom cabinets away from the stone that comprised the kitchen wall and swept up the nest. Then I worked the place over with bleach. Deer mice are notorious carriers of hantavirus, ehrlichiosis, and babesiosis. A small percentage carries the bacteria that causes Lyme disease, even in Arizona, and many deer mice host the fleas that carry bubonic plague, which was discovered in Arizona as recently as 2020. I set snap traps behind the counter and more outside the back door. I placed the traps on paths that hugged the house walls, which the package proclaimed was the route preferred by three out of four mice. At first, I set one trap per day, and then two, and then three. My morning routine—often before coffee—involved pulling on work gloves and popping mice from the springs, dropping their corpses over the back fence to feed local scavengers.

Then the outside traps started disappearing. A trap I set on an evening was missing by morning. I looked in the vegetable garden under the tomato plants. I searched under cholla and mesquite. I examined entrances to underground burrows for signs of something that had been dragged. Not a trace.

The telltale sign of a pack rat is a midden, which is a heap of sticks and cactus pads and other desert detritus. The word *midden* is an Old World term for "pile of shit." Pack rats cement the sticks and garbage together with their viscous urine, which crystalizes over time. As long as a midden is kept dry, which is easy to do in the desert, it remains intact. Middens standing four feet high and four feet wide have been found in the Grand Canyon dating back to the Pleistocene 50,000 years ago, which is as far back as radiocarbon dating goes. These middens have become the measure of choice among scientists for comparing ancient vegetation with modern plants to see how far we have evolved as masters of the universe.

A suspicious pile of sticks and prickly pear fruit almost two feet high leaned next to the woodpile just outside the back fence. I have learned that inside a midden, pack rats build bedrooms separate from the kitchen. Some even have separate bathrooms, although I can't see the point, given the viscous urine used as building material. Females live in the bigger, more conspicuous middens, which serve as nests for many generations. Middens in prime locations are often occupied for centuries and ruled by the family matriarch. When she dies, the nest is inherited by the dominant daughter. In other words, my rats weren't going anywhere by choice. If a substantial percentage of a rat population is eliminated, the remaining rats have more sex and increase their reproductive rate to try to catch up. They play to win.

Pack rat nests are also home to kissing bugs. Attracted to porch lighting and carbon dioxide, kissing bugs like to bite sleeping people on the mouth and then defecate near the bite. Although typical human reactions to a bite from a kissing bug can vary from none to anaphylactic shock, these insects carry the parasite that causes Chagas disease, which manifests as enlarged heart, altered heart rate, heart failure, cardiac arrest, enlarged esophagus, or enlarged colon. One source told me that kissing bugs can't bite through clothing and suggested pajamas as a solution. I don't know about you, but when I do wear pajamas, I don't usually wear them over my mouth. I believe a more effective defense against kissing bugs is to eliminate pack rat nests.

When I drove to the Walmart on the Mexican border to buy more mouse traps, I spied a rat trap on the shelf. I hesitated when I held it in my hand. Something about the heft of it made me think of a guillotine and created visions of the blood and guts that would await me if it actually worked. I reminded myself that my beef was with the mice invading my kitchen, not the rats cozy in their midden outside my boundaries. I put down the rat trap but added a large jar of Skippy extra creamy peanut butter to my shopping cart. Back home I set the mouse traps around the perimeter of the house and devised a plan if I found evidence that I really did have a pack rat. I called a friend in Portal, a retired biologist, who had done field work with small mammals and was comfortable in their company. I asked to borrow his Havahart live catch trap, knowing that if I caught a pack rat, I would be forced to pick up a cageful of live, scared, defensive rodent. My friend offered to bring the trap over to my place that weekend, and to my relief promised to help me release the rat if I were lucky enough to catch one. I was certain that releasing a rat five miles away in Cave Creek Canyon would put enough space between us that it would no longer be my problem.

That evening, just as it was getting too dark to see, a gray shadow under a pine just outside a glass door caught my eye. It wasn't moving. Until it did. I grabbed my binoculars to get a better look, although it was just ten feet away. It was a white-throated woodrat (*Neotoma albigula*). Long naked tail. Round back, head down. Every now and then it jerked. In the dim light I tried to focus on a bit of it in order to conjure the whole. Then I saw the mouse trap on its head. The weight of the trap on its head held the rat close to the ground. Compared to the size of the pack rat, the mouse trap looked like a hat. A dunce cap.

Can you feel sympathy for a rat? How much? I told myself I was sorry for its misery, but it was too dark and too late for me to do anything about it. Surely the creature would be dead by dawn. Maybe it would just disappear. Isn't that how these things work? I've often wondered why I don't stumble across more dead birds or coyote skeletons or lizard bones. Where do they all go? I convinced myself that wild animals choose to die out in the wilderness where no one is watching, perhaps guided by some primordial need for privacy, the same instinct that for millennia has led them to hide their suffering or signs of weakness.

I considered briefly the possibility that it might not die on its own and envisioned the ways I could kill it. I could drop it into a plastic garbage bag and tie it tight and deposit it into the trash bin. I could bludgeon it with a shovel. I pictured myself lifting the shovel high overhead and bringing it down with a whack on its back. Or I could pick it up with the shovel and drop it in front of my car and then run over it. The other option was to do nothing and let nature run its course; passivity can be just as deadly. I feared by doing nothing I was only extending its misery. More importantly, nature hadn't put the mouse trap on the rat's head. I did.

The rat lay still and I prayed it would be dead by morning. I asked myself who I thought I was praying to. Wasn't my god also the god of rats? And who do I become when I pray for the death of an innocent creature?

The light was rapidly diminishing, but through the binoculars, I could see the rat's face. Its eyes were the color of San Simon obsidian, a natural glass used by the first inhabitants of the valley as tools and weapons. Reflected in that glass was the same fear I felt but on a much different scale. I was afraid of the rat; the rat was afraid for its life. My impulse to kill it rose from all I thought I knew about disease, destruction, and self-defense. But my ability to kill followed a reverse ratio in relation to the mass of the rodent, from mice to rats to prairie dogs to capybaras. As far as I could tell, the amount of effort required to exterminate an animal grew in direct proportion to its size, which is why I found it easiest to smash ants and spiders, relatively simple to snap off mice, but impossible to kill a larger mammal. The proverbial slippery slope and all. But I was beginning to realize that the real difference was that unlike bugs I could squash in an instant, unlike the mice who died in snap traps at night in the dark, this rat was suffering and I was its witness. When I looked again several minutes later, I could no longer see the rat. The night had absorbed all the shadows.

The neuroscientist Dr. Jaak Panksepp discovered in 1999 that rats giggle when tickled. Panksepp and his team actually used their fingers to tickle lab rats on their tummies and recorded the chirps they made. When slowed down enough for human ears, the chirps sounded like expressions of joy. Panksepp and his team also found that the rats in their experiments enjoyed these encounters and sought out the researchers' hands in order to play with them. I knew none of this the night my pack rat was suffering. I only recognized the pain I had caused. Which raised the question: How far would I go to save a rat?

The next morning the rat was still alive, covered with ants. Angry at being forced to make a decision and act on it, I called my friend the biologist. At first I hesitated, concerned that the tone of my voice would make me sound like a woman incapable of dealing with the tough things, the things that make me squeamish. On one hand, I was disappointed in myself for not handling a situation of my own doing. On the other hand, I was repulsed exactly because it had been my own doing. I told myself I wasn't depending on a big strong man—I was seeking professional help. "I don't need your Havahart trap after all," I said and explained the situation. "What do I do? I want it gone but I don't want to torture it."

I was grateful that he didn't laugh at me or say, "It's a pack rat, for god's sake." I was especially grateful when he offered to come over and take a look.

Twenty minutes later we both stood over the rat, staring at the trap on its head. It was the first time I had looked at the animal without a window between us. Up close it seemed less scary. Up close it was just another living being trying to survive.

"Do you want to save it?" he asked. His tone was inscrutable; I couldn't tell if he was making fun of me or showing empathy. I figured that at this point it didn't matter.

"Is that possible? I mean, does it have a chance?"

I made no effort to move or to help in any way. I no longer cared if the rat lived or died. I only knew that if the trap had snapped its neck and killed it immediately, I wouldn't have been standing there with a stone in my heart.

My friend had brought work gloves and a small towel. As he approached the rat, it began thrashing with everything it still had. We were both surprised it had that much energy left. When he threw the towel over the rat, it stilled. He picked it up with its head facing away, although with a mouse trap on its head, there was no way the rat could have bitten anyone.

"Where do you want it?" he asked.

On some level, I must have understood that the rat would die. I didn't suggest carrying it far away so it wouldn't return. Instead we found a place outside the fence about a hundred yards away, under a creosote bush. He pulled back the hammer part of the trap and released the rat from its grip. He gently placed the rat in the shade. "It might make it," he said as we walked away.

In a perfect world, the rat would summon its strength to scamper off and join the myriad other pack rats in the desert. It would grow up with a cautionary tale to tell its relatives in the gene pool. It would twist my desire for the death of this rat upside-down.

In a really perfect world, I would never use snap traps again. But when mice began reappearing in my vegetable garden and the zucchini and tomatoes that I had spent time and money cultivating began disappearing, I bought another jar of peanut butter and set new snap traps. This time I was careful about where I placed them; I set a couple inside the wire fence that outlined the garden and placed small-gauge wire cages directly over the traps. I attached mesh to places along the garden fence where I thought pack rats could get in. And I tried to plan for my karmic future by never killing spiders again. I caught any spider or other bug inside the house under a plastic jar, which I inverted and carried outside. When I released the spider on the ground, I half expected it to run to the mice to remind them about our deal—leave my food alone and I won't feed the mice to the coyotes—but the spiders mostly seemed stunned upon release, as if incredulous about their luck.

If the rat lived, I hoped it had learned its lesson. Maybe I would learn a lesson, too. Maybe I would see that I didn't go far enough, didn't act soon enough, didn't care deeply enough. Because I believed that rats were responsible for the tiny flea or germ that could cause me pain and illness, although the chances were remote, I believed that rats were evil. I had unconsciously allowed the rat to remind me of my own vulnerability. I had flipped the position of power from me to the rat and it unnerved me. If the reminder of mortality was subconscious, the realization that I had turned into an animal abuser was painfully obvious. Perhaps the answer was not buying into a hierarchy of orders of life but reaching an insight of interconnectedness—even with a rat.

That conclusion was not easy or perfect, given the snap traps I kept in my vegetable garden and under the hood of my car. As a compromise, I bought my own Havahart trap and prayed to the gods of mice and men that if I ever caught another pack rat, I could find the courage to deal with the things that scared me.

I checked on the rat a few hours after my friend the biologist had placed it under the creosote. It lay dead where we had laid it. Within days its tiny carcass had disappeared.

Hammer Test

Imagine a spectrum of living creatures. At one end are viruses, bacteria, paramecia. Add invertebrates like worms, snails, octopuses, and shrimp. In the middle, find spiders, crabs, and small animals like frogs, snakes, and songbirds. Somewhere toward the opposite end stand the bigger creatures like prairie dogs, house cats, wolves, alligators, and whales. Holding down the far end are humans—not because of their size or evolutionary superiority, but because of their claim to a moral code. Now picture yourself holding a very large metaphoric hammer that can take many shapes—revulsion, fear, hunger, defense, medical research, vivisection, euthanasia, capital punishment. That hammer represents your willingness to kill. How far along that continuum will you bring your hammer down? Squashing a bug is probably okay, especially if it is a spider or a cockroach or other creepy crawly that freaks you out. And you might be willing to catch a mouse in a snap trap if it's in your kitchen, eating the crumbs in your dark corners. If you're an omnivore, you let others butcher your dinner, unless you fish or hunt your own food. Where do you draw the line about killing living things, whether you actually do the deed or support others doing the killing in your name? According to national Gallup and Pew polls, fifty to sixty percent of American adults go all the way to support the death penalty. Where do you stop?

I was unsure of my own answer to that question, especially when I considered threatened species and their preservation. In a natural world made unnatural by human intervention, I questioned the limits of my ethical responsibilities. In my view, a species doesn't need to provide an obvious benefit to mankind—or even to the rest of the natural world—to be worth saving. Its value lies in the mere fact of its existence. I have heard it said that allowing a species to go extinct is like ripping pages out of a book that you are still reading. When we are the cause of that extinction, the blame for that loss is ours to accept or ignore. What was I willing to do, either actively or passively, to affect the outcome one way or another?

The first good look I had at an American bullfrog in the Chiricahua Mountains was in the sights of a .22 rifle. I had accompanied a biologist and his field technician—let's call them John and Bob—to a pond that had potential to be a safe harbor for Chiricahua leopard frogs. John and Bob had been monitoring this pond in the flatlands east of Cave Creek Canyon for months. This morning the two men started at the bottom of a pond and counted eyes as they circled to the top. They estimated more than five hundred bullfrogs. They knew the frogs were bullfrogs and not leopard frogs because their size and the chirp they made when they jumped into the water were dead giveaways. John and Bob were on a mission to eradicate some bullfrogs. I found it ironic that they needed to kill a frog to save a frog.

With hundreds of bullfrogs living in this flatlands pond, it was obviously not yet ready to receive the leopard frog tadpoles or egg masses that were ready for release. Tasked by U.S. Fish and Wildlife to eradicate the bullfrogs that make life impossible for Chiricahua leopard frogs, John and Bob intended not to kill every American bullfrog in southeastern Arizona, but to establish a buffer zone around Cave Creek where the leopard frogs could thrive. If Chiricahua leopard frogs can't be returned to their entire previous range, they can at least be saved from extinction. The first step was to give them a suitable home.

Before I came to the Southwest Research Station in the Chiricahua Mountains in 2016 to learn about the reintroduction of Chiricahua leopard frogs to their homeland, I had read that Chiricahua leopard frogs and American bullfrogs are incompatible. Perhaps that's not the right word—"incompatible" makes it seems like they argue a lot or have different political views. But a bullfrog will eat a leopard frog tadpole—and an adult leopard frog, too, if the bullfrog can fit its mouth around it. They also eat other bullfrogs. In southeastern Arizona, others of their own species are the most common vertebrates found in the guts of a bullfrog.

Chiricahua leopard frogs were already in trouble before they encountered any bullfrogs. Biologists estimate that in the early 2000s, Chiricahua leopard frogs inhabited only about fourteen percent of their historic range in Arizona and New Mexico, although no one knows for certain if that is an accurate guess. Leslie Canyon National Wildlife Refuge, close to Arizona's borders with Mexico and New Mexico, persisted as one of the last remaining places in the state where Chiricahua leopard frogs still occurred naturally. Extreme drought conditions from 2009 to 2010 stopped the flow of Leslie Creek through the Swisshelm Mountains at the south end of the Chiricahua Mountains. By 2011 only a few shallow pools remained. That's when biologists from several organizations stepped in to initiate a captive breeding program to try to save the species. They gathered fourteen leopard frog tadpoles from Leslie Creek and transported them in vats to the Southwestern Research Station in Cave Creek Canyon, where the species had been identified in 1979. They planned to establish a new population of leopard frogs, but first they had to deal with their bullfrog problem.

To some residents of eastern North America where the American bullfrog is endemic, its croak epitomizes the warm nights of lazy summers. Those nostalgic folks might be less inclined to romanticize the bullfrog if they knew that it is considered one of the worst invasive species and one of the top predators in the world. Fittingly, a group of frogs is called an army.

Bullfrogs thrive in part because they tend to dominate their environments to the detriment of other species. Another reason is because female bullfrogs lay up to twenty thousand eggs at a time. New studies show that after an American bullfrog hatches, it develops individual characteristics based on what it learned about its predators while it was still an embryo. When bullfrog eggs exposed to the smell of predatory fish morph into tadpoles, they hide more effectively than tadpoles that never smelled a predator while they were still eggs. These tadpoles mature into cautious frogs; they grow longer, too, suggesting that unlike leopard frogs, some bullfrogs are born more prepared to adapt to a changing environment.

After they are established in a region, bullfrogs are difficult if not impossible to get rid of. Native to eastern North America, bullfrogs were introduced to the American West during the California Gold Rush, when they were raised for food to supplement a miner's meal of beans, bacon, and bread. A female bullfrog can weigh almost two pounds; her legs are the prime portions. By the late 1920s bullfrogs were common along the Colorado River near Yuma, Arizona. No one can say how the bullfrogs reached the river, although they can travel up to six miles across land in just a few weeks.

During the Great Depression, desperate farmers took up raising frogs for food and for niche markets like biology labs and specialty leather. A 1936 edition of *Popular Mechanics* encouraged readers to start a bullfrog farm in their backyards. All you needed to do was write to the American Frog Canning Company for a copy of *A Fortune in Frogs*, a "big, illustrated frog book" that "explains our money-making proposition in detail." An Arizona website, still online, sold bullfrog tadpoles for $1.99 "per item" if you bought a thousand or more, although it no longer allows you to put bullfrog tadpoles in your cart. But this "family owned and operated facility since 1987" still claims that because bullfrogs eat mosquitos and other bugs, they are ideal for your backyard pond and will become an important part of your ecosystem. They offer no advice on how to keep your bullfrogs from running away.

American bullfrogs have spread or been introduced to more than forty countries across four continents, either intentionally or accidentally, but always successfully. In many countries, escaped pet bullfrogs gave rise to feral populations that have overrun native species. Some countries—France, China, Taiwan, and Venezuela—imported bullfrogs as food and turned the less appetizing individuals loose in public parks and ponds, where they proved to be voracious. In Colombia, bullfrog farms have evolved into a biological plague. Bartenders in Singapore serve a concoction called Royal Hashima Dessert made from dried fruit and hashima, which are a female frog's oviducts. Practitioners of traditional Chinese medicine insist that hashima is good for your lungs and skin. In 2016 Singapore was consuming an estimated 15 million frogs a year, presumably by happy, healthy drinkers with great complexions.

Although I have never ordered a cup of Royal Hashima Dessert or eaten frog legs, I understand that it is an exaggeration to suggest that frog meat (like rattlesnake, rabbit, and crocodile meat) tastes like chicken. Diners, especially French ones, enjoy eating frog legs, but chefs are less enthusiastic about cooking them. Bullfrogs are notoriously hard to clean because the skin is slippery, rubbery, and tough. The cook at the Southwestern Research Station told me that the biologists suggested that for Halloween dinner, she could serve the bullfrog legs they had collected; the walk-in cooler that held the frog legs stank like a swamp for a week afterward, she said. You can barbeque, stir fry, and deep fry frog legs. I have come across recipes online using canned frog meat for stuffed baked apples and American giant bullfrog cocktails, a kind of ceviche with catsup. The French like them coated with milk and flour; folks in Louisiana eat them stewed in a gumbo and served with a picante sauce. The Halloween partygoers enjoyed them fried up with horseradish.

Months before I held that .22 in my hands, I had seen my first Chiricahua leopard frog at Cave Creek Ranch. The unassuming amphibian balanced on the bank of a pond rimmed with spike rushes and dotted with fallen sycamore leaves. It wasn't love at first sight, but that's because I had such high expectations. I wanted my first leopard frog to indicate in some way that she was a survivor—that she proudly carried the banner for success at a time of extirpation of many species, not just her own. I was counting on a tiny amphibian to assuage my guilt for my role in dooming her species, a hero who realized that she represented hope for the future of life on our planet. I didn't know how a frog would demonstrate that, exactly, but I wanted something more than a hunchback smaller than my fist. Instead, as I approached, my frog hopped off a rock and made a sharp turn underwater. She resurfaced minutes later, with only her bulging eyes peeking above the surface of the water, her body hidden under a clump of algae. Evidently she wasn't terribly impressed with me, either.

It was hard for me to reconcile such a fuss over such an unremarkable creature. I had read that one of a Chiricahua leopard frog's distinguishing characteristics is its mating call that sounds like a two-second snore. Is that what convinced wildlife managers from various public and private organizations to design an ambitious reintroduction program? Was it the spark that brought this little frog to someone's attention, which led to the realization of their decline, and then ultimately to the goal of saving the species? Where do I see value? Where do you?

A string of ponds stretches like pearls along nine miles of Cave Creek Canyon, from Ash Springs in the mountains at around six thousand feet to Cave Creek Ranch at the canyon's entrance, where

I spied my frog. As part of the Partners for Wildlife program, the Southwestern Research Station together with Arizona Game and Fish and the U.S. Fish and Wildlife Service dug this series of ponds on the eastern slope of the Chiricahua Mountains. The owners of these private properties agreed to "contribute to the recovery of species listed as endangered or threatened under the Endangered Species Act." In exchange for their conservation work, the landowners' responsibilities toward an endangered species do not expand beyond that agreement, which is especially appealing to those who see the Endangered Species Act as government overreach. I find it hard to wrap my head around the argument that privileges personal property rights over the preservation of a species. Opponents of the law argue that it mandates changes to the way landowners manage their land, which can be inconvenient and costly. I believe species—even unremarkable, snoring frogs—are priceless, and their loss is more than inconvenient. The debate is another example of a chasm that only seems to widen; rather than finding middle ground, each side becomes increasingly entrenched. I suppose I am as guilty as anyone else. But regardless of their politics, Partners for Wildlife gained a small riparian refuge complete with dragonflies, native plants, and leopard frogs.

This pond at Cave Creek Ranch was the first pond dug to launch the reintroduction effort. Those fourteen original Leslie Canyon tadpoles eventually morphed into hundreds of frogs eager to reproduce. Five years and several egg mass transfers later, dozens of adult leopard frogs lay suspended in the pond at Cave Creek Ranch. The mid-April weather was just warm enough to encourage the leopard frogs to emerge from their cozy homes in the winter mud and enjoy the rising water temperature. Leopard frogs get their name from the brown spots on their green backs. When the temperature of the pond reaches an agreeable degree, the frogs can turn as bright green as a newly leafed-out sycamore. Their camouflage serves them well under a water surface that reflects the overhanging tree leaves.

My second sighting was a pair in amplexus. Unfortunately, I hadn't heard the mating call snore; I only caught sight of its fruitful outcome. The males are much smaller than the females and this guy had grabbed his girl around her armpits; he hung off her back end, fertilizing the eggs she was releasing. They didn't move—there was no thrashing around or humping or pumping—although it looked as if the female might drown under the weight of the male. After several minutes, the pair jerked and spasmed with a splash, the male still riding the female, still holding on for his shot at immortality.

The adults were surrounded by hundreds of tadpoles, all heads and wiggly tails. Some tadpoles had sprouted tiny back legs, although they still had their tails. To me, all looked healthy, although illness in a frog is hard to spot.

Chytridiomycosis is a disease caused by a parasitic fungus known as *Batrachochytrium dendrobatidis* or Bd. It has infected most of the world's estimated 6,000 amphibian species and has led to the decline of 500 species and more than 90 extinctions. In addition, more than thirty percent of the world's frog species currently are in danger of extinction. A 2023 Aquatic Conservation paper said Bd could possibly extirpate entire populations of amphibians and already has driven certain species to extinction. A paper published by The Ecological Society of America in 2022 stated that chytrid "caused the greatest recorded loss of vertebrate biodiversity attributable to a pathogen."

Frogs are harbingers of trouble in two environments. They live on both water and land, soaking up pollutants from water through their jelly-like eggs, and absorbing toxins as well as water and electrolytes from the air through their permeable skin. The skin of a frog infected with Bd thickens; the electrolytes accumulate until the frog can no longer breathe or thermoregulate. Ultimately, the frog's heart stops. In a matter of weeks, an entire frog population can be decimated by chytrid, which tends to target rare native species. In susceptible species like Chiricahua leopard frogs, even a low dose of chytrid can be fatal. American bullfrogs, on the other hand, are immune.

As I circled the pond at Cave Creek Ranch, adult Chiricahua leopard frogs jumped from rocks and grasses to join the tadpoles swimming in the water. The more closely I looked, the more tadpoles I spotted in various stages of their journey to adulthood. Metamorphs are tadpoles in the process of development, which continues for several weeks. Their mouths expand to the width of their heads, and they replace gills with lungs to breathe air instead of water. A pair of tiny front feet pop out from under an individual's skin to complement its developing back legs. It grows a long tongue that is attached in the front instead of the back of its mouth. The frog graduates from being a vegetarian to being a carnivore, living on moving prey and consuming many times its body weight in insects. The rate of a tadpole's development depends in part on the temperature of the water; the warmer the water, the faster the transformation. In this pond, ten to twelve weeks after hatching from an egg mass, they resembled frogs with tails. Three to nine months after hatching from an egg, a frog's evolution is complete.

We are not that different from frogs. We share a phenomenon known as apoptosis, where living cells cause their own death. All cells with a nucleus are capable of this kind of self-destruction; cells that were once essential become unnecessary. A tadpole loses its tail; a human female loses the lining of her uterus during her menstruation every month. The process is tightly controlled, programmed within the cell; it cannot be stopped or reversed once it is initiated. Life becomes possible only through death, even in a single cell.

In the research station cafeteria, before we went out to survey the pond overrun with bullfrogs, I had asked John how he felt about doing his job. Did he feel any regrets for the thousands of bullfrogs he had killed? Did he ever get emotional when he pulled the trigger?

He seemed wary of me, as if I might misconstrue his intentions even if he could explain them. He held my gaze for a second longer than comfortable, trying to interpret my own intentions. He seemed confident in his understanding of his role but reluctant to give too much of himself away. He didn't answer me directly. "You need to come with us and see for yourself," he said.

Which species adds more value, bullfrogs or leopard frogs? In 1973 the Endangered Species Act acknowledged that endangered and threatened species "are of esthetic, ecological, educational, historical, recreational, and scientific value to the Nation and its people." Under this law, U.S. Fish and Wildlife is legally responsible for helping species survive. For Chiricahua leopard frogs to thrive, someone needs to take action. It is too late to let nature take its course; humans long ago bent the environment to our liking. Little in nature is natural anymore. If we caused the problem, are we responsible for its solution? If we keep interfering—especially if we don't—will we have anything left that's wild?

My only point of reference was a similar dilemma with an entirely different animal. In a parallel attempt to save a vanishing species, barred owls were being eradicated in Oregon. The plan was ultimately to kill 3600 barred owls. Barred owls are an eastern species that has overrun the last remaining habitat of the northern spotted owl. Without a safe place to call home, spotted owls will disappear. The biologist responsible for ridding one small forest on the West Coast of barred owls said that the first time he pulled the trigger on his 20-gauge shotgun, he had to steady himself against a tree because he became so emotional. Some animal rights advocates call the idea a conservation program from hell. Other conservationists call the alternative a guaranteed extinction of the spotted owl. Either way, something must die so that something else can live.

Some folks argue that extinction is nature's way of moving on. But the rate of decline of the worldwide amphibian population is now more than a thousand times what is considered normal based on fossil evidence. After existing on earth for more than hundreds of millions of years, some frog species survive only in zoos. Since 1980 more than 160 amphibian species have vanished; in the same amount of time, five bird species and possibly two mammal species have gone extinct. No one knows exactly how many species have died out because losses are poorly documented, research is difficult and often takes place in remote places, and the computer modeling that estimates are based on uses a wide range of variables. The most easily accounted for are the vertebrate animals that comprise about one percent of all known species. New species of mammals, birds, reptiles, amphibians, fish, and insects are still being discovered.

When we arrived at the property, Bob hopped out of the SUV to open the ranch gate. John drove through and parked close to the pond. They circled the perimeter of the pond, counting bullfrogs, then returned to the SUV, popped the hatch, and opened their gun cases.

I watched the two men get ready to do their job. "I don't know if I could do it—shoot a bullfrog," I said. I was still skeptical, uncertain of any decisions I would make if I were in their shoes. The thought of killing frogs of any species in any way made me squirm. But if I'm honest, I'm not exactly innocent, if I count the various spiders, bees, flies, mosquitoes, and mice that I have killed over the years. Why exactly was I squirming?

"Have you ever shot a gun before?" Bob asked as he raised his rifle from its case.

"No," I replied.

We walked to the edge of the pond, and Bob held his rifle sideways in front of me.

"Are you right-eye dominant or left-eye dominant?" he asked.

"I think I'm left-eye dominant."

"Oh, well, this rifle is set up for right-eye."

"In that case I'm right-eye dominant." I suddenly understood that I was about to find out exactly how I felt about shooting bullfrogs. My enthusiasm surprised me; I worried I was betraying what I had believed about myself just five minutes earlier. I came fully alert.

"This is the safety," he said, pointing to the button that toggled from side to side. "Push it to the left and the safety is on. Push it to the right and it's live." He moved the button back and forth to show me how it's done. I heard the click each time. "This plastic bag is tied on here to catch the spent casings."

He put the rifle in my hands and pointed it toward the water. It felt surprisingly light as I pushed my hat up on my forehead and leaned my right eye against the scope.

"Ready?" he asked. He placed my index finger on the safety and repeated what he had shown me, pressing the button with my finger. "That way is safe. This way is live."

I nestled the butt close against my shoulder. "Is this going to raise bruises?"

"No," he said. "There is no recoil with this gun."

It took some adjusting to see clearly through the barrel of the scope with no unfocused edges obscuring my view. After I moved my head around until my vision aligned through the lenses, a bullfrog came clearly into view. It looked directly at me. I placed the intersection of the crosshairs under its chin.

"When you have it in your crosshairs, push the button to unlock the safety," Bob said. "Remember to breathe. And squeeze the trigger on the exhale."

I exhaled. I squeezed. The bullet exploded out of the .22. The pond spit out something that looked like a rubber toy. It landed with a splash. I had killed my first bullfrog.

"You got it," he said, smiling. "There's another one to the right. Do you want it?"

My reaction was automatic, fueled by adrenaline and a surprising sense of righteousness. I found the answer to what I was willing to do. I was as sure as I had ever been about anything.

"Oh yeah," I said, exhaling.

I got my second bullfrog on the first shot, too, but by the third bullfrog, I was shaking so hard that I couldn't see straight through the scope. My entire body vibrated with the thrill of hitting my target; the rush was overwhelming. Bob said I had buck fever. "It's what deer hunters get when they're so excited they miss," he explained, taking the rifle from my hands. I wanted to argue that I hadn't missed—I could no longer see straight through the scope but took the shot anyway. I knew that if I had been able to focus, I would have gotten that third bullfrog. I was disappointed and wanted to try again, although I realized it was time to stop.

My high was underscored with the gratification that comes from accomplishment. I understood I had weathered some kind of test, although I wasn't sure if I had passed or failed. I wasn't considering the two dead frogs now floating in the water. More important, I wasn't thinking of the fact that I had killed my first creature other than those random bugs and mice. I felt no satisfaction in having contributed, in however small a part, to the advancement of Chiricahua leopard frogs as a species. I was aware of only a shockingly strong surge of power and control. I felt proud and clever and victorious. And very surprised.

By virtue of a deeply visceral response, I had come down on the side of killing a member of one species so that two species could persist. In the battle between Chiricahua leopard frogs and American bullfrogs, the only available options are to kill American bullfrogs directly or kill Chiricahua leopard frogs indirectly. We are responsible by doing something, and we're responsible by doing nothing.

Is this what it feels like to appreciate an opposing point of view—about extinction, or the value of the natural world and our role in it, or land use or politics or any other thing? Can killing beget empathy? The sparks that flew as two conflicting concepts rubbed up against each other electrified the way I thought. I got hooked on the high—that brilliance, that flash of revelation, was something I wanted to experience again. If opening my mind and heart to another way of thinking could cause the rush I felt at the edge of that pond, understanding and tolerance of different opinions could become a habit. It might even grow to become contagious, targeting infectious concepts. The idea is exhilarating.

The Nature of Mutability

A pictograph of a long-horned bison (*Bison latifrons*) spreads across a cave wall in the Alamo Hueco Mountains, a limestone escarpment in the New Mexico bootheel eight miles north of the Mexico border. Evidently a thousand years ago or more, an Archaic hunter was so impressed he painted an eight-foot image of the beast, solid black in a pigment made from oxidized iron, on the cave's back wall. But bison weren't completely eradicated from New Mexico. One story goes that a wild herd of *Bison latifrons*'s modern descendants, American bison, believed the grass was greener on the U.S. side than in northern Mexico. About a hundred years ago, the herd trampled the old border fence separating New Mexico from Sonora as if political borders were merely lines drawn on a map. I've heard that bison are still living on that ranch in the New Mexico bootheel.

I stood on an eastern flank of the Chiricahua Mountains, on the Arizona side of the Arizona/New Mexico border. Gold and orange polka dots that were this spring's poppies climbed the western slope of the Peloncillo Mountains on the New Mexico side. In between the mountain ranges, the state border ran north and south through the San Simon Valley. I had trouble picturing bison grazing here; this desert landscape didn't match the typical plains habitat where bison roamed in my imagination. The valley sported circles of farmland made productive through the use of center-pivot irrigation. When they were introduced in the mid-1900s, these systems revolutionized labor-intensive family farming that relied on hand-dug irrigation channels.

Over time, however, this irrigation method sowed the seeds of its own counter-productivity; as the center-pivots grew more water-efficient, farmers irrigated more land and planted denser and thirstier crops, until in some places entire aquifers eventually were depleted. In my line of sight, the green crop circles were conspicuous against the dusty brown land where cattle grazed. Adobe casitas and single-wide trailers cluttered the view. The incongruity of bison grazing through this landscape, even as it might have looked a thousand years ago, skewed my vision of what was possible.

Straight downhill and slightly to my right stood a copse of deciduous trees—the remaining trace of an ancient ciénaga, a water source for the early people who called these mountains home. I could make out a small, cleared area, about a hundred yards long and the width of a one-lane dirt road, covered with native bunchgrasses. In 2016 the bones of six American bison were discovered in this peat-covered site, known as the Cave Creek Midden. Although now-extinct long-horned bison and ancient bison (*Bison antiquus*) roamed the plains of North America hundreds of thousands of years ago, archeological evidence shows that American bison (*Bison bison*) appeared in the Southwest only ten thousand years ago. Radiocarbon testing dated the bison bones from Cave Creek Midden to be about three thousand years old. Because they found no butchering or cooking tools, archaeologists believed the animals got stuck in mud and, unable to escape, slowly died.

White-crowned sparrows whistled and curve-billed thrashers sang from the slope behind me. From my left on the valley floor, I heard only the crackle of straw-colored grasses swaying with the breeze. I recognized it as a field of Lehmann lovegrass—*Eragrostis lehmanniana*.

I laughed with a snort as I said the words out loud. The botanist who named the genus in 1776 left no record of how he came up with the name. Speculation about its origin has included a theory that the flower tops got caught in women's skirts and crept upward along their legs. Another theory was that the word *eragrostis* came from the

Greek *eros* meaning "love" or *era* meaning "earth" and *agrostis* meaning "grass"; the suggestion was that the flower tops had a characteristic "female aroma." These ridiculous suppositions prove only that more women need to get into science. No matter its origin, "lovegrass" is a benevolent name for an invasive plant that transformed the landscape by outperforming the native species and began the grasslandification of southeastern Arizona.

I tried to picture this landscape green with native grasses, before Lehmann lovegrass blanketed the area with what in fall appears as quintessential amber waves of grain. A native of South Africa, Lehmann lovegrass sports feathery spikelets in a herringbone pattern on top of two-foot-tall stems. When its stems are eaten by grazing cattle, the plant quickly replaces its culms and most of its leaves by using energy stored in its roots. The variety was introduced in the Southwest U.S. to feed cattle, another invasive species, which had been brought to the Americas in the seventeenth century to feed the most invasive species of all.

Lehmann lovegrass has already outperformed many native grasses over much of southeastern Arizona, making survival more difficult for local wildlife. Its seeds are too tiny for most insects to eat, resulting in fewer resources for grassland birds that feed on either or both seeds and insects. Only one bird species, Botteri's sparrow, has continued to nest in stands of Lehmann lovegrass, although meadowlarks also will nest there if their only other option is not to nest at all. Loggerhead shrike, horned lark, Cassin's sparrow, grasshopper sparrow, savannah sparrow, vesper sparrow, hispid pocket mouse, pygmy mouse, western harvest mouse, and nine species of grasshopper have decreased their numbers in grasslands dominated by Lehmann lovegrass. Only fulvous cotton rats and one other species of grasshopper have thrived. On the annual bird counts I have been participating in for the last ten years on the Arizona/New Mexico/Mexico border, I have watched bird population numbers dwindle, especially among sparrows. On the 2018

Portal, Arizona, Christmas Bird Count, a total of sixty-six chipping sparrows were seen by all observers; four years earlier, the count was three thousand five hundred and fifty-one.

I looked through my binoculars for signs of roosting barn owls at the ciénaga, but the only animal I saw was a local dog. I tried to picture what was now invisible—the ancient people who lived here, intimate with this landscape, hunting a succession of progressively smaller mammals like deer and rabbits as the water evaporated. The groups of people who lived in this part of the American Southwest have been given various names by historians and anthropologists—Clovis people, Pueblo people, Mogollon culture. Over millennia, their lifestyles adjusted to their surroundings, as I imagine my habits and those of my neighbors must adapt as the climate and the landscape continues to change.

Archaic subsistence morphed into dry farming; pre-contact irrigation systems still used today brought agricultural opportunities. Cattle were brought to the New World around the time Spanish conquistadores captured Tenochtitlan and Tlatelolco. By the mid-1500s, herds of skinny corriente cattle spread across Mexico almost as fast as the growing numbers of Spanish colonialists the cattle were slaughtered to feed and clothe. Missionaries, miners, and ranchers, all looking for their own version of fortune, pushed north and multiplied, pulling their animals behind.

Capitalism, opportunism, and innovations from barbed wire to cow towns led to the cattle ranching boom in the American Southwest. The Spanish government and then the Mexican government granted land to any pioneers who would settle the area; southern Arizona's biggest cattle ranches evolved from these land grants. When silver was discovered in southern Arizona in the 1870s, prospectors, miners, and merchants came seeking their fortunes, and new breeds of beef cattle picked up a hungry market. Cowboys and vaqueros worked intricate cattle drives to bring longhorns from overgrazed pastures in Texas across New Mexico to the seemingly empty Arizona grasslands. Before refrigerated railcars allowed cattle to be shipped to Chicago's meat packing plants, the animals were raised primarily for their hides and tallow. As the railroad pressed West and the population grew, the federal government bought huge quantities of beef to feed soldiers stationed at new U.S. Army posts built to protect settlers from Apaches determined to take back their land.

By the 1890s, there were about one and a half million cattle in Arizona—about seventeen head to every person. Cattle needed grasses and grasses needed water, a scarce and valuable commodity in this desert. Here, water is money; large cattle operations devised schemes to monopolize the available resources. Farmers fought the ranchers seizing the water sources and the cattle destroying their crop fields; Native Americans objected to cattle outcompeting the game animals for the scant resources. As cattle ranching grew into a profitable national industry, more rangeland was opened to grazing and competition for resources intensified. By the end of the nineteenth century, ranchers had seriously damaged the land through the southern Arizona practice of grazing more cattle in good years than could be supported in order to ride out the bad years. The land responded to the introduction of huge herds of domesticated, commodified cattle by growing less resilient, like a dispirited response to a viral attack.

I was too new to the area to recognize the changes that occurred here over time. From the ridge I scanned the valley, trying to envision the landscape before cattle grazing, when bunchgrasses rather than mesquite covered the ground. I imagined the early white settlers, especially the women who moved here in the nineteenth century. What did they see when they arrived? Did the desert surprise them, as it did me when I first moved here, as it still does? I tried to picture the San Simon Valley filling with cattle, the transformations that surrounded the settlers who had no concept of what had been normal here before them. The imaginations of the men who drove their families' covered wagons must have been filled with visions of wide open spaces and the promise of opportunity; the women no doubt expected a safe place to raise their children and a life of hard work free from the grime of the city.

From where I stood on this side of the ridge, I saw no cattle or cattle ranches, although I knew some of my neighbors on Sulphur Canyon Road raised livestock. Instead I saw other homeowners like me on lots of forty acres or more. All had been here longer than I, with more stories to tell. Locals referred to a tenderfoot like me as a "newbie" who brought an outsider's values to a place run on the customs of settlers, who in turn displaced Native populations who valued their own traditions. I knew the words "invasive species" caused some old-timers to prickle with indignation, although I didn't know how the long-time ranchers might define the term. I figured they might use it to refer to newbies like me. I decided to have a conversation with some local cattlemen about Lehmann lovegrass.

Jim Frank Cox and his wife Shirley were my neighbors, which meant they lived about three miles away, as the raven flies. (All distances around here are measured as if birds fly in a straight line; the roads in this county are circuitous, rarely going directly from point A to point B.) One sunny day I arrived at their ranch house at the end of a winding dirt road named after Mr. Cox's grandfather, Frank Sanford. Mr. Cox and an old ranch dog greeted me at the side door and led me into the kitchen, where he shared his memories, happy for the company and my interest.

Born in Portal, Arizona in 1938, Mr. Cox had been a cowboy all his life; for eighty years he moved and fed livestock, gathered and branded calves, monitored and mended fences, all from the back of a horse. "There was cattle everywhere" from the Chiricahuas to the Peloncillos, he told me in his gravelly voice. As we sat at his kitchen table, he described his years as a day worker. Like his father and grandfather before him, Mr. Cox worked for various ranching operations, including the Z Bar T, the Red River Cattle Company, and the San Simon Cattle and Canal Company. "I don't call it a hard life," he said, pausing to spit juice from his chewing tobacco into a cup. Because there were no other jobs available, once a year he would drive cows and their calves to Rodeo, New Mexico, a distance of about ten miles. There the calves were loaded onto cattle cars and shipped out on a train that was always late. He supplemented his annual roundup paycheck with the $30 a month he could make by moving cattle from Slaughter Ranch on the Mexico border to a holding camp outside the town of San Simon, a several-month operation that required fifteen or sixteen cowboys, a cook, and a couple of wranglers.

Ranching in Mr. Cox's family goes back to 1889 when his great-grandfather brought his three young sons and his mother to the Chiricahua Mountains. The family arrived in a wagon from Sweetwater, Texas, encouraged in part by the Homestead Act, which promised 160 acres to citizens willing and able to complete five years of continuous residence on the land. As Mr. Cox explained it, "They had to change the law because 160 acres is not enough to make a go of things here. Eventually, you could buy a section, which is 640 acres." Alternatively, a settler could pay $1.25 an acre to buy the land after only six months' residence. No matter which way you acquired the property, you were required to "improve" the land by cultivating it and building a house on it. Mr. Cox's great-grandfather homesteaded 640 acres, his grandad homesteaded 160 acres, and his father homesteaded the adjacent 640 acres.

What did this valley look like in his great-grandparents' time? I wondered aloud. How did the landscape adapt to the cattle? And how did the grasses evolve, especially with the introduction of Lehman lovegrass?

"On my ranch I could see six different types of native grasses," Mr. Cox recalled, naming six weeks grama, sideoats grama, black and blue grama, five-finger grass, and Arizona cottontop. "The grass grew as high as my stirrups," he said before adding, "But you can't talk about grasses without first talking about weather."

I knew that in this part of the country, talking about weather meant talking about rain—and the lack of it. Severe droughts in the 1890s began a cycle of dry periods followed by wet spells that lasted until 1930. Overgrazing eroded the topsoil from the rangelands; the native grasses never grew back. By 1930, more than half the cattle in Arizona had died of starvation.

Given this history of the land, scientists began to look for inexpensive, easy-growing forage for cattle that had already eaten all the grasses that grew here naturally. In 1932 a South African botanist named Dr. Maria Wilman identified Lehmann lovegrass as a species that could revegetate the badly eroded San Simon watershed. She sent some seeds to Dr. Franklin J. Crider, the horticulturist who served as the first director of Boyce Thompson Arboretum in Superior, Arizona. As she predicted, Lehmann lovegrass soon demonstrated its potential to revive the grasslands in the desert Southwest.

In the 1940s a retired dentist devised a method of broadcasting pelleted Lehmann lovegrass seed from his airplane, questioning only how to sow the introduced species at scale and not whether it was a good idea. Because lovegrass grows best in areas with sandy loam soil, rare freezes, and summer rainfall totals of six to eight inches, it did spectacularly well in the desert grasslands and shrublands of southeastern Arizona, especially along highways where the seeds are scattered by passing vehicles. The Arizona Department of Transportation began seeding Lehmann lovegrass in 1965. In twenty years they had seeded 4100 acres, mostly along Interstate 10 between Tucson and the New Mexico border, Interstate 19 between Tucson and Nogales, and Highway 80 between Rodeo and Douglas. The planted areas were not grazed for two years to allow the new seedlings to become well established. A 1984 issue of the *Arizona Farmer Stockman* announced that "Lehmann lovegrass can now be considered a naturalized citizen." By 2003 Lehmann lovegrass was the dominant type of grass on more than 1.4 million acres across southeastern Arizona rangeland, dramatically altering the environment.

Mr. Cox admitted that without Lehmann lovegrass there would be more native grasses, but he was quick to point out that not all native grasses are good. In his opinion, "Burroweed is the most invasive species." He was referring to a foul-tasting herb with yellow flowers (*Isocoma tenuisecta*) that lives on southern Arizona's dry slopes and mesas. Mr. Cox had a bone to pick with burroweed, he said, because it contains tremetone, a toxin that can cause severe muscle tremors he called "the trembles" in the legs and muzzles of animals, especially horses. Some animals never completely recover; some die.

Mr. Cox left this valley only once—to work in Missouri and California for a few years. He returned in 1989. By that time, the valley had changed in ways he found hard to come home to.

"Portal had been 'discovered'" Mr. Cox said, using air quotes around "discovered." When he moved back onto his family's ranch in 1958 with his new bride, "there weren't forty registered voters" in Portal, he said, adding that "none of these houses that you see today were here." When I asked what had been here, he described the fate of three ranchers who "… got sold out. Their land was split up into these forty-acre parcels that were being built on."

His eyes got serious for a moment when he described what he saw as the decline of the way of life this valley supported in his great-grandfather's days. "I don't think a lot of people that come here care, really, to know this." He waved his hand as if to clear the air between us. "For one thing, there was a lot of people like yourself that come in from back East that didn't understand the people here and what had gone on in the past. How come there's deeded land for you to buy? Because

somebody roughed it out for years to get a patent on a piece of land."
He pointed out the window. "My grandparents homesteaded right over
there, a hundred yards from here, in tents. One of the tents that their
beds were in burned down, burned all their clothes and their bedding.
People went through all kinds of hardships to settle this country. This
is a hard country."

I was guilty as charged. Born and raised in Chicago, I had lived
in big cities all my life. I moved to Portal on a whim, looking for a
home that offered clean water, clean air, and hiking out the back door;
I had bought one of those forty-acre parcels Mr. Cox scoffed at. I knew
nothing of the recent history of this area; that was why I was sitting at
his kitchen table. On the other hand, Mr. Cox showed no awareness
of the people who lived here before settlers arrived, or perhaps he just
didn't want to talk about it. Each of us in our own ways, whether we
choose to acknowledge the past or ignore it, changes the landscape by
building a life on it.

High rates of births and immigration in the early nineteenth century
fueled a population explosion in the U.S.: from 5 million people in
1800 to more than 23 million by 1850. Two economic depressions
contributed to the reasons millions of Easterners journeyed west in
search of new land and opportunities. They didn't always recognize
what they saw when they arrived. Land they considered vacant was
actually home to bands of Native Americans, who suddenly had to deal
with strangers eager to stake claims and make "improvements."

"There's four generations of us buried in Rodeo," Mr. Cox said.
But the Chiricahua Apaches who were removed from this land by the
U.S. Government in the 1880s might disagree with his assessment that
he belongs to this valley. Two centuries before the first Europeans came
to this area, claiming authority granted by God and king to conquer
all they "discovered," communities of Picosa Culture peoples called this
part of Arizona and New Mexico home. Look beyond the Pleistocene
and the record gets sketchy. The archaeologists who explored Cave

Creek Midden established that the site defines the Middle Archaic period, one of the least understood but most important prehistoric eras in the American Southwest—from the time humans colonized the desert borderlands around 4000 BCE to the time they introduced agriculture around 2100 BCE.

The San Simon Valley holds its memories of the cattle that grazed here and the grasses that grew here, as well as all the people who have walked this earth: Ancient Puebloan people, Chiricahua Apaches, Spaniards, Mexican and American settlers, ranchers, farmers, researchers and scientists, retirees, and me. As the world's human population continues to explode (according to the United Nations Population Fund, human population shot from 1.6 billion to 6.1 billion in a hundred years), as habitat for multitudes of plants and animals dwindles, as species go extinct because of the changes we force upon the planet, we have become the most dangerous species.

Some cattlemen I talked with were quick to defend Lehmann lovegrass. One long-time rancher claimed he could manage Lehmann lovegrass better than he could manage dirt. Another old-timer declared that one man's degraded prairie is another man's improved pasture.

When I sat down with Ted Troller, a rancher in Portal, to have a conversation about grass, he warned me not to jump to any conclusions. "Cattlemen will tell you about the advantages of Lehmann lovegrass," he said, comparing it with native grasses. "There's less erosion, it needs less water, and it seeds easily."

Like Jim Frank Cox, Ted Troller had been ranching and farming in the Chiricahua Mountains for more than fifty years and took over from his father, who worked the land for fifty years before that. We chatted one evening in his living room on the AVA Ranch. Mr. Troller was twelve years old in 1952 when his family bought the ranch, which he described as "a few miles wide and several miles long." After naming some of the perils of cattle ranching in the fifties and sixties, including deadly threats from pink worm and screw worm, he explained that cattlemen sowed Lehmann lovegrass intentionally on their rangeland for forage.

Mr. Troller said he planted "a lot of grass" in 1990 on a test plot of land in Cave Creek Canyon. He irrigated the plot from a ditch that had been dug by hand in 1911 by neighboring families; the ditch ran almost three miles from Cave Creek. He learned that he could produce six thousand pounds of grass per acre, "which means that you can carry over a hundred cows per section. And per section today, we're looking at, in most of this country, maybe ten cows per section." He leaned back into his big armchair. "It doesn't make sense unless you have something that makes a lot of money."

But money has never been his only consideration. Mr. Troller once turned down an offer from Paul McCartney to buy the AVA Ranch. "What would have happened if I sold to Paul McCartney? What would Portal look like today?" he asked, raising his eyebrows in anticipation of an answer. His question reminded me of a presentation prepared by R.E. Rosiere, Professor of Range Management at Tarleton State University as well as a cowboy with a sardonic sense of humor. Professor Rosiere disparaged "city slickers who drive recreational vehicles, join the Sierra Club, and solve the problem of Lehmann's lovegrass invasion by converting the natural vegetation into crabgrass monocultures sandwiched between paved streets and cul-de-sacs." As it turned out, Mr. Troller's fears were unfounded. Rather than buying the AVA Ranch, Paul and Linda McCartney bought a 151-acre ranch on the eastern edge of Tucson near the Tanque Verde River; to this day, that area of the Rincon Mountains foothills retains its desert landscaping.

When I asked what he liked about Lehmann lovegrass, Mr. Troller replied that it sprouted earlier in the year and stayed green longer than most native grasses. Half of what cattle eat in the spring are the tender shoots of Lehmann lovegrass, he said. In dry summers, it produces almost four times more forage than native grasses. But in an average summer as the stalks mature, cattle only lightly graze Lehmann lovegrass; presumably, the grass isn't as appetizing when it gets older. Its nutritional value is greatest in winter when its protein content is higher than that of many native grasses, making it especially important to lactating cows. He added that Lehmann lovegrass can be grazed heavily and, unlike native grasses, doesn't need rest.

I pointed out that Lehmann lovegrass was invasive, but Mr. Troller put a different spin on my information. "Lovegrass is not pushing out the native grasses. It's just more successful," he argued, neatly sidestepping the cost of that success or even its definition. Some measure success in economic terms; some value traditions that evolve over time. Others value a balance between human advancement and the health of an ecosystem.

When I mentioned the changes this valley has seen, especially in native and introduced species, Mr. Troller challenged me to define my terms.

"Well, what's native?" he asked, shooting me a stern look.

This is not a simple question to answer. Some definitions say that a native species evolved in a given location; if it evolved somewhere else and was brought to a new location, it is considered introduced there. The USDA defines native plant species this way: "Only plants found in this country before European settlement are considered to be native to the United States." For a plant species to become established in any location, it needs to adapt to changes and successfully reproduce. But at what point does too much adaptability become the problem?

I didn't get the impression he was expecting me to answer. He also didn't offer his definition of native, which was fine with me. I reminded myself that I was a newbie and a guest in Mr. Troller's home. I sensed that some kind of cowboy courtesy was preventing the conversation from going steeply downhill. I decided it was time to get an opinion that was as close as possible to being impartial.

"I don't strive for a perfect future, just a possible one," Doug Ruppel would tell me when I visited him in his office, just four miles north of the Arizona/Mexico border. As the U.S. Forest Service District Ranger in Douglas, Arizona, Mr. Ruppel has no dog in this fight; his statement was probably as unbiased as I was going to get in this corner of the state. He had been in the ranching business for twenty-six years before getting a master's degree in rangeland science and joining the U.S. Forest Service about ten years ago. When I emailed him on a Sunday afternoon to ask if he had time to talk about current management of grasslands in Cochise County, he replied within an hour and suggested a meeting the next afternoon.

During my fifty-five-mile drive south to Douglas on Highway 80, I passed long strips of Lehmann lovegrass along the edges of the highway. I stopped the car to collect a specimen for Mr. Ruppel to confirm what I was seeing. Lovegrass has a dense mat of roots that bind it to the ground, which is what makes it effective for erosion control. The plants I grabbed refused to yield to my tugging, tearing through my hands until the stalks finally broke loose at the base.

I rubbed my palms and looked up into a cloudless sky. On the horizon to my left, I spotted a small herd of pronghorn up against the Peloncillo Mountains, across the state line in New Mexico. A North American species (not an antelope) that survived a mass extinction 11,000 years ago, their numbers declined drastically in the early twentieth century, prompting state-wide programs to redistribute animals to ranges like this one that can support new populations. Like the bison they were often hunted with, pronghorn are herbivores, eating sagebrush and forbs; the bones of both have been discovered in caves in the area, indicating that they were a source of food for early people. The cave with the bison pictograph was about forty miles due east from where I stood. Whoever had painted that homage to the bison must have known, or at least hoped, that the image would remain long after the artist was gone and possibly long after the bison had disappeared.

Was the artist's vision born of a faith that things would always be this way or did a premonition of things to come spark the painting?

The pronghorn grew uncomfortable with me being in their line of sight and galloped farther east before stopping and turning their large heads to look back. I knew they could walk for miles, unobstructed by anything manmade other than the occasional wire fence that they slip under rather than jump over. (Cattlemen who care about these things use unbarbed wire for the bottom strand in their fencing). After a few minutes, the pronghorn ignored me and continued to graze in fields where there were no crabgrass monocultures, no subdivisions, no paved streets or cul-de-sacs. I appreciated the open vistas and was surprised to feel unexpectedly grateful to the ranchers who had roughed it out for years here, standing against multiple pressures from outside interests—developers, conservationists, investors—that grew as cattle ranching waned. It was easy, albeit misguided, to feel as if time stood still here.

Mr. Ruppel placed my lovegrass sample next to a large pile of paper on his desk. He described Lehmann lovegrass as an opportunist with "a seed bank in the soil and a wide window of time" to germinate. It can sit dormant for years before it grows to "fill a hole in the mosaic of a range area." But the spread of Lehmann lovegrass is not a natural progression, he said, pointing out that it doesn't invade healthy stands of grass. He reminded me that Lehmann lovegrass was introduced at a time that this country was feeling the effects of the Dust Bowl, when soil conservation was still an unknown science. "It was brought here by man and introduced without knowledge of the consequences," he said, before concluding, "But now it's here and it isn't going away. We can only manage it in a way that does the least harm."

I thought again of those nineteenth century women who moved out West to a land that probably surprised them. I remembered when I first arrived here and stared with awe into the mouth of Sulphur Canyon behind my cabin—the same canyon those settler women witnessed, the same cliffs and rock formations the Clovis people saw when they raised their eyes from the hunt. It's the feeling that has been catching my heart every time I return to the Chiricahua Mountains.

I turned my attention back to Mr. Ruppel, who was saying that "fire, drought, and grazing pressure have reduced competition from native grasses." I was beginning to recognize that even grasses fight for dominance and compete for resources. As Mr. Ruppel described the steady progression of Lehmann lovegrass across Arizona rangeland and the role climate change plays in its acclimatization, I realized the competition will only get more fierce.

"Climate change has changed how the models work," he said, referring to the state-and-transition models developed by the USDA Natural Resources Conservation Service to illustrate ecosystem dynamics. "We have sped up things that took eons to impact ecosystems." As the area becomes hotter and drier, favoring Lehmann lovegrass, there will be "no co-evolution of native grasses, which haven't evolved in its presence—they have only been out-competed," he said. "Local ecosystems will find a balance, but maybe not in our lifetimes," he added, seeming resigned as he concluded that Lehmann lovegrass "is not going away."

I walked out to the parking lot where my car sat baking in the shade of the only tree. As I waited for the steering wheel to cool off enough for me to touch it, Mr. Ruppel's comment about ecosystems finding balance reverberated. I sat in my car running through a list of all the counter-arguments I could have made and considered, for just a moment, going back inside. I thought again of the bison bones at Cave Creek Midden and suspected that Mr. Ruppel might consider species going extinct an "imbalance" while it is actually a fact of life and death over the cycles of nature in an ongoing, interdependent world. When he commented that resilience comes from diversity and asked, "Has man's hand on the landscape made the environment more resilient?" I could have returned a question of my own: "Isn't resilience just nature correcting our human-caused imbalances?" Adaptability is a learned response; adapt or go extinct, I could argue. To be one of the lucky ones who successfully adapt to a changing world, I need to rethink my assumptions about my relationship with the land while maintaining my sense of wonder, keeping my mind and heart open to respect what is here before it is gone. What I could have said to Mr. Ruppel is that the concept of the balance of nature should be replaced with a term more relevant to our times: the mutability of nature.

On my drive back north on Highway 80, I spotted Lehmann lovegrass in places I hadn't noticed before. My reactions alternated between admiration of waves of straw-colored fields to concern about a dangerous invader. As I neared the parcels of forty acres and more at the entrances to Horseshoe Canyon and Sulphur Canyon, I sensed the ghosts of ranchers measuring me with contempt and pity and recognized I had been doing the same toward them.

Researchers predict that the warming climate will drive Lehmann lovegrass farther north. Some climate scientists predict that entire ecosystems will begin to migrate as the climate warms and water becomes scarcer. When I think of migration, I think of mammals and birds and bands of people. I reminded myself that ecosystems— including rivers and valleys and mountains—are also living things, although they live on an immensely larger, immeasurably slower scale.

I lowered the window of my SUV and inhaled the scent of creosote and ozone; I scanned the fields for sparrows and meadowlarks but saw none. I suddenly had an unnerving premonition of this valley, in its stretch between these two mountain ranges, looking nothing like it looked at this moment. I saw the bison come and go, the lovegrass extend and disappear, and all us humans—just another species inhabiting this land—become ghosts, leaving behind only painted images of what we considered important during our brief lives here. I saw bones emerge from the desert floor, polished white by the sand and heat. I saw new possibilities filling new voids. A soft breeze made me blink; when I looked again, I saw only heat shimmer.

One Creature Among Many

There is a species of ant that steals babies. These raiders attack other ant colonies, abduct the young, and raise them to be workers who do everything for their captors.

When *Polyergus topoffi* ants go on a raid, they look for a nest full of young *Formica gnava*, their close relatives, to kidnap. The Formica ants grow to become adults, which takes only a week or two, and remain among the Polyergus colony for the rest of their lives, doing the same things they would have been doing in their Formica colony—feeding the queen, caring for the new young, tidying up the chambers and tunnels in the nest—only they're doing it for a species in a different genus. The Polyergus colony becomes so dependent on these workers that they are incapable of caring for themselves. They can't feed themselves and won't even take food unless it is regurgitated into their mouths by a worker. They'll starve to death instead. Is it slavery? parasitism? adoption? brainwashing? or a form of cooperation unrecognizable to humans?

One summer evening in southeastern Arizona's Chiricahua Mountains, I hiked through the Coronado National Forest with Howard Topoff, the animal behaviorist for whom *Polyergus topoffi* ants are named. Apache pines and alligator junipers formed the canopy overhead; pine needles and leaf litter softened the ground. Howard, a friend in

Portal, was taking me to see what he called a slave raid. He explained that underground, inside an undefended nest, Polyergus raiders pick up the naked, cocoon-less pupae in their sharp mandibles well suited for fighting and carrying off captives, but worthless for anything else. E.O. Wilson, the legendary Harvard entomologist and colleague of Howard's, wrote that evolution has transformed Polyergus ants "into specialized fighting machines capable only of conducting efficient slave raids."

The vulnerable pupae stolen from the Formica nest are in the stage between larva and adult, between looking like a maggot and being a bug with six legs, two antennae, and a waist so delicate the adults easily snap in two. Unable to move on their own, pupae are completely defenseless. They are as big as grains of jasmine rice—the same size as the Polyergus adults who stumble home carrying the booty in their jaws. The raiders deposit the pupae in a Polyergus nest, which originally was a Formica nest, to be cared for by Formica workers who think they're Polyergus, and grow up dedicated to ensuring the survival of a species not their own. It is a little confusing but I think of it this way—it's as if a troop of vervet monkeys broke into a local pet store and carried off all the newborn Labradoodle puppies. And the puppies grow up feeding and cleaning up after their monkey family because that's the only reality they've ever known.

Humans shape our beliefs according to how the world affects us personally. Ants, on the other hand, are unique in their lack of uniqueness—they live in communities with no concept of the individual. They don't self-reflect and wouldn't contemplate their navels even if they had navels. At least that's what we know at this point in our science. Chemicals guide their behavior, not trust or optimism or conflict avoidance. Not hate or love or politics.

When Formica ants emerge from their pupae state (a process known as *eclosion*), they fully believe they are Polyergus ants. Or as Howard put it, "As far as the Formica ants are concerned, they are not slaves, they're adopted. It's a matter of identity, and how individuals define themselves."

It seemed to me that it's more of a variation on identity theft. Polyergus ants don't steal the identities of the Formica ants; they steal the ants themselves and then impose their identities on their captives—as if Polyergus realize they are one of the rarest species of ants in the world and are trying to compensate somehow, with a misguided understanding of speciation. A world of mystery and intrigue that I hadn't noticed was happening under my feet—until I took a walk with Howard.

A Polyergus queen leaves her home nest only once, to mate for her first and only time. She emerges from her underground home into a strange world of sunlight, fresh air, and warm summer breezes and releases a pheromone that attracts swarms of male ants, who have also just emerged from the nest for the first time. A lucky male or ten mate with her in the middle of a swarm that turns into a raid, or a raid that turns into a swarm. It's hard to know the difference.

Known as a *drone*, which in another context can mean *unmanned*, a male ant lives just to inseminate a queen. That's all the males do, and when they're done, they're dead. A male ant can't return to his home nest because the female worker ants won't let him inside. And he can't try to join another colony because he will get eaten. Most male ants die of exposure after their brief moment of bliss. E.O. Wilson and Bert Hölldobler, who cite Howard's research several times in their seminal work *The Ants*, observe, "Within a few days of eclosion… the males have been quickly converted into single-purpose sexual missiles."

Howard explained that because Polyergus ants are unable to care for themselves, the successfully mated (the biologic term is *fecundated*) queen needs to find an existing Formica colony to raise her eggs. The Polyergus queen enters the tunnel of a Formica nest and hurries past frenzied workers to locate and kill the Formica queen. All ant queens have a signature chemical, like a brand of designer perfume. After killing the queen of the colony, the raiding queen then licks off the dead queen's scent.

Who knew ants have tongues? I wondered, imagining a Polyergus queen lapping the perfume from the body of a Formica queen.

Within fifteen minutes of killing her rival and stealing her scent, the Polyergus queen is accepted by the Formica workers who pledge their allegiance and dedicate their lives to her care. The labor force of an entire Formica colony exists to ensure her reproductive success.

The pheromones that a Polyergus queen steals are still effective a week after she kills the host Formica queen. She will spend the next twenty years doing nothing but laying thousands of eggs in the nest she has conquered. Every egg is produced from the sperm the queen has stored from her single day of sex. She will never leave home again.

Did I mention that all ant workers are female? And there is no king?

Other than the queen and the handful of short-lived males who develop from her unfertilized eggs, all ants are sterile females, who live out their lives in service to their queen. Some workers forage for food—a dangerous job that often ends with the forager becoming the meal rather than finding it. Others serve as nurses to the larvae or as ladies-in-waiting to the queen. Some older females stand guard near the nest entrance and are the first to rush to the defense if the colony is attacked. Wilson and Hölldobler wrote, "It can be said that a principal difference between human beings and ants is that whereas we send our young men to war, they send their old ladies."

On an otherwise nondescript slope of the forest floor, Howard spotted the wooden marker he had placed a year ago to flag a Polyergus nest.

The ants were hard for me to see even after Howard pointed them out. He cleared away some sticks and stones to get a better look at the throng that appeared to my untrained eye to be writhing in confusion. They all looked the same to me, so I asked Howard how he could tell which species is which. He replied that if you opened a mixed-species ant mound and uncovered distressed red ants and unruffled black ants, you could be pretty sure you found slave makers—the red *Polyergus topoffi* ants—and slaves—the black Formica ants. Formica adults have shiny heads and bodies; the dullness of the adobe mud color of a Polyergus adult's skin (called the *cuticle*) makes her compound eyes even more conspicuous as they sit unblinking and unmoving in her head. A Formica adult's shorter antennae, which both species hold out from their heads at the same right angle, bend closer to her head. The workers in both species are roughly the same size, which is tinier than the garden ant that enters my kitchen uninvited on warm summer days.

Without a Formica queen producing more Formica eggs, the mixed-species Polyergus colony needs another way to replenish its labor force. When the colony reaches a certain size, the Polyergus ants resume their raiding, commandeering more Formica pupae to care for the growing population. These raiders are always Polyergus; Formica ants never go after their own kind. It's the only job a Polyergus worker will perform.

Raids are started by scouts. If a scout finds a suitable target colony, she returns home to mobilize the raiders. The scouts share their good news, inciting workers to emerge from the nest in an enthusiastic tumult before collecting into a column to organize a sortie. The procession leaves behind a pheromone trail to help them find their way home when they are laden with booty so large, they can barely see past their antennae. According to Howard, a Polyergus colony can consist of 2,500 raiders and up to 6,000 slaves. They can steal as many as 2,000 pupae from a Formica nest during a single slave raid, but a typical number is closer to 600. Over a summer's raiding season, a

Formica colony can lose 14,000 pupae; replenishing the supply will keep a surviving Formica queen busy all winter.

During a raid, hundreds or thousands of Polyergus ants pile into the target nest. The frightened Formica ants scatter immediately, without stopping to rescue their brood. Howard explained that the lack of defense is caused by a panic-inducing pheromone that is not secreted by the invading Polyergus raiders, but by the frantic Formica workers themselves. As the Formica workers run away higgledy-piggledy in response to the toxic pheromone, the Polyergus raiders, who are immune to the formic acid, methodically pick up the Formica pupae, carry them home, and drop them at the nest entrance. Formica slaves bring the pupae underground to their Formica sisters. Ants injured in the raid are eaten.

With his white hair and beard, Howard looked like a cross between Charles Darwin and Merlin the Magician, both of whom he often dressed as, usually when lecturing about the natural world. Merlin has also been known to appear at nonspeaking engagements during holidays in the Portal, Arizona community, to the delight of kids of all ages.

Darwin wrote about watching ant raids in the 1850s and suggested that slave-raiding evolved when ants stole more pupae than they could consume. Pupae that weren't eaten soon eclosed and accepted their captors as family. Ant scientists (*myrmecologists*) theorize that slaves form social bonds with their captors as a result of what a pupa smells when it ecloses. The first thing a Formica pupa smells in a Polyergus nest is the odor of Polyergus ants, which it immediately identifies as its own. Once they become slaves, Formica ants no longer recognize the young of their own species.

Individual ants brand other ants as outcasts if they don't like the way they smell. These foreigners are often aggressively kicked out of the colony. But ant slaves are much less likely to become aggressive toward ants outside their home nest. Research shows that kidnapped ants raised in mixed colonies are exposed to a greater diversity of chemical cues and learn to be more tolerant of others. This exposure reduces the ants' ability to distinguish foreign versus home-nest individuals and makes them less inclined to attack the host ants they are supposed to be serving. The diversity-rich social environment changes the behavior of the enslaved ants.

So what evolutionary purpose does slavery serve in the animal kingdom? Darwin, who called slavery "this truly wonderful instinct," had no answer. "How the instinct first originated of taking slaves, we are left to conjecture," he wrote.

It might help to understand that evolution is not an inexorable march toward progress and think of it instead as the temporary success of a species adapting to its current environment. With success as the measure, ants are considerably more evolved than humans, given that there are at least a million and a half ants on the planet for every human being. Some scientists predict that insects will survive us all. But conjecture about the future is more of an art than a science these days, as the rate of change accelerates as a result of human interference with the environment. The more I learned about the underground secrets of ants, the more I hoped the planet was holding on to a few more surprises. I also hoped those surprises would be pleasant.

Most scientists will tell you that evolution isn't a competition and that no one wins the evolution game, which is really all about survival. To be successful in survival, sometimes all it takes is an evolutionary idea. Howard said there is no way of knowing anything about the first successful raids, "but some queen got away with the idea once, and the rest of the colony just ran with it."

As we waited for a raid to commence, I asked Howard if he thought the terminology used when discussing this stuff is outdated. Terms used by entomologists when discussing Polyergus ants is appropriated from the worst of human behavior. The term *slavery* when discussing ants is considered controversial in some circles and not only because it is offensive. It's not even accurate. The kidnapped ants are not exactly slaves because no one forces them to do anything. The queen isn't much of a monarch, Howard pointed out—she doesn't rule subjects, give orders, or wear a colorful crown. In fact, she doesn't do anything at all except lay eggs and get waited on. But in Howard's view, she did invent "a unique method of finding childcare."

Some educators say that the term *slave* can cause students to think twice about entering the field of biology, not only because of the history of human slavery, but also because the field is dominated by men immune from it. The preferred scientific term is *dulosis* from the Greek word for *slave*, but I don't see how that is any better. It's the same word translated; the idea remains the same, only disguised to anyone who doesn't read Greek. Ironically, the word *Polyergus* is Greek for *hardworking*.

Even the terms *colony* and *society* carry weight. All ants are social—there are no solitary ants. The proper term to describe Polyergus ants is *eusocial*, which means they cooperate for the benefit of the community. Ant societies divide big jobs into small tasks individual ants can perform; working together, an ant colony can move mountains, or at least what seem like mountains when they start their jobs. The colonies depend on this cooperation for their survival.

Howard has written, "As far as anyone has been able to determine, socially parasitic relationships between ants do not offer any benefits to the slave species." All relationships between slaves and hosts are unilateral. That is, one party benefits and the other suffers.

These were difficult concepts for me to wrap my head around. If ant slaves suffer, it seemed reasonable to me that they would revolt. But they don't. Unlike Polyergus ants, who have completely lost the ability to be anything other than parasites, Formica ants can survive outside the colonies where they are enslaved, although they choose to emancipate themselves only when colonies grow overcrowded. Like humans, their reaction shows that stress can be a powerful change agent.

Howard explained that the slaves never revolt because they are more like workers with autonomy. The queen relies on her female workers to do everything for her, including raising her offspring to become slave raiders who perpetuate the cycle, allowing the colony to prosper and grow. As long as there has been life, species have used other species to their advantage.

"Human civilization has its origins in our ability to use other species to provide food and labor," Howard has written, "in the process we call domestication." Humans have domesticated other animals, including sheep, chickens, and goats, to use as food, similar to the way Formica slaves consume some of the Formica pupae carried home to the nest by Polyergus raiders. Humans use domesticated horses, donkeys, and camels as beasts of burden. But humans are the only species that have enslaved members of its own species.

When it comes to understanding ant behavior, I can only talk about ant societies with my human vocabulary based on my human ideas. Are ants mindful of a shared agreement, a pact made among sisters? As I watched the ants moving about the entrance, I couldn't help but wonder if they consider their behavior "cooperative." Do they put a value on themselves and their work?

I tried to envision a world run by a clever, industrious group of females who get things done without complaining. Myrmecologists argue passionately about whether this behavior implies altruism. They cite the example of the evolution of worker ants who give up the ability to reproduce in order to ensure the future of their species, which sounds counterintuitive but actually works pretty effectively for large ant colonies. When individuals forgo their own gain for indirect benefits to the entire species, what have they sacrificed and what have they won? How often do human individuals, in societies that prioritize self-expression and fulfillment, sacrifice for the good of the community or even for the survival of the species?

Polyergus topoffi ants go on raids after the heat of a summer day, typically between five in the evening and dusk. Howard watched the raids every summer not far from his home in Portal. But we didn't see a raid on our walk through the forest in the Chiricahuas. In fact, Howard hadn't seen one all summer. For the first time in thirty-five years, Polyergus wasn't raiding. Howard blamed it on the recent years of drought, which reduced the number of Formica ants in the vicinity. Howard predicted it will take several years for the colonies to come back.

Recent headlines have proclaimed the declining numbers of animal populations. For example, by 2019, populations of vertebrates crashed by an average sixty percent, and bird numbers were down twenty-five percent. Giraffe populations have fallen forty percent in thirty years, and a species of river porpoise is decreasing more than thirty percent every decade. In 2017 researchers discovered that insect abundance in Germany, as measured by biomass, declined by more than seventy-five percent over twenty-seven years. But it's hard to get a precise headcount of specific ant populations. I don't know if anyone has measured the rise or fall of the numbers of *Polyergus topoffi* ants in the Chiricahua Mountains, but I'm willing to bet the numbers have fallen, not risen. I watched the lethargic Polyergus ants outside their nest and worried about how long the drought would last. Already rare, Polyergus are sensitive to disturbance in their environment, which puts them at even greater risk in this time of climate crisis. Their complete dependence on their hosts increases their chances of extinction. I considered the

Formica ant nests I hadn't seen on our walk. I wondered if either species will ever recover.

It's easy to think of ants as pests more than contributors to the ecosystem, especially because to most observers, ants are ubiquitous busybodies that are not as fruitful as bees, for example, or as good-looking as butterflies. But ants are essential workers that we literally couldn't live without—they condition soils, disperse seeds, and control the pests that can destroy us, like mosquitoes and ticks. Ant colonies favor interdependence over individualism, cooperation over self-promotion. Their cooperation has made ants one of the most successful life forms on the planet.

I stared at the ants on the ground until their movement became an active pattern among the arrangements of the leaves and pine needles. What had seemed chaotic flipped into an elegant display of the power of what had seemed before to be small or insignificant.

My Eight-Snake Day

The keen winds that sweep the valley between the Chiricahua and Peloncillo Mountains can make slithering along the ground on your belly seem like a reasonable way to get around. Spring and fall gusts can wobble mere humans, but snakes just hug tighter to the ground. Like prickly pear and cholla, snakes are icons of the southern Arizona landscape. Thirteen of the sixteen species of rattlesnakes in the U.S. live in Arizona. But even out here in the sun-bitten intersection of the Sonoran and Chihuahuan deserts, where snakes are as common as dust devils, eight snakes in one day caught my attention.

Not all the snakes I saw that October day were alive, and not all were rattlers. At sunrise I noticed movement in the pine outside the bedroom window. A four-foot Sonoran whipsnake—a greenish-gray nonvenomous snake with a white underbelly and a slender head—was making a vertical ascent along the trunk, using only friction and muscle to cling to the bark. It was a remarkable accomplishment, considering that neither the trunk nor the snake had limbs. I watched awestruck until the snake settled into a crotch of the tree, level with the tiny balcony off the second-floor bedroom. Minutes earlier I had been sleeping twenty feet away with the glass door open wide. The fact that snakes could climb trees caught me by surprise. I knew from this day forward I would move through the world differently, watching under my feet and above my head simultaneously, reevaluating what is safe.

Ophidiophobia. Fear of snakes, which can manifest as that queasy feeling at the thought of being close to one, or worse, actually touching one. The belief that snakes are slithery, slimy creatures that are better dead. Not all snakes are dangerous, although their reputation suggests otherwise. The world's largest religions blame the serpent for the original couple's eviction from paradise; Christianity, Judaism, and Islam all cast the snake as a shrewd liar who promised Eve that through her loyalty, her eyes would be opened. By realizing their capacity for evil as well as good, the couple became more human. There is no reason to blame the snake for its knowledge of our most basic nature.

On that October morning, I carried an early breakfast of toasted homemade bread with farmers' market jam to the back patio that faced the canyon. I sipped black coffee and watched shadows melt down the Chiricahua Mountains in Arizona as the sun rose behind me over the Peloncillo Mountains in New Mexico. Liquid orange poured down from the Chiricahua ridgeline, spilling over boulders and crags, painting the face of Portal Peak. It was a spectacle guaranteed to impress, and it occurred every morning.

I limited myself to a single cup of coffee to get ready for another spectacle—the annual international quarter horse race in a corner of the Malpai Borderlands that straddles two states and two countries. Before the border wall and before Homeland Security money funded an extravagantly oversized facility on the border at Antelope Wells, just a five-strand wire fence divided New Mexico from Mexico. Every October, visitors on both sides enjoyed a program of two-horse races along a dusty quarter-mile track. In each race, one Mexican horse and jockey raced one American horse and jockey, with the fence running between them. The riders were local cowboys and the horses were working quarter horses and cow ponies. There was no betting window, no public address system, no photo finish replay. Pesos and dollars exchanged hands; punters gathered at the finish line to call the dead heats. After the results were settled over a beer or tequila, it happened again for the next race.

Malpai. A bastardization of "mal pais," the Spanish words for "bad country." A terrain known as desert pavement, formed after centuries of wind scour off layers of sand and dust, leaving a smooth crust.

I tore myself from the view to grab the laundry from the washer. Here in the desert, I took advantage of the heat and hung my clothes on a line strung between poles behind the house. When you're carrying a full laundry basket, it's hard to see your feet. A gopher snake, however, had a clear view of me. It had ventured from underneath the house and curled into a cozy coil in front of a clothesline pole. Gopher snakes are friendly, nonvenomous snakes that do an excellent job of rodent control. They also perform a brilliant impression of a rattlesnake when they are about to get stepped on. There is no mistaking that sound—I could hear it even as I screamed, dropped the basket, and sent wet clothes flying.

I reflexively reached for the snake stick I bought on eBay. The contraption resembled one of those devices designed to help shopkeepers retrieve a small item from a top shelf—a long aluminum pole with padded calipers at one end, which you closed by squeezing the handle at the other end. I kept it handy during snake season from April to October. The end of the season, August through early October, is the snakiest time, as baby snakes—neonates—venture out on their own and adults scout for enough food to last through hibernation. I positioned the tongs behind the snake's head and squeezed gently while carrying the hapless snake outside the yard. Still shaking, I gathered up the muddy laundry.

Defensive behavior. A protective response to a perceived threat. A scared gopher snake can hiss loudly enough to be heard above any ambient noise, like boots on gravel or wet laundry falling from a basket. The snake can also vibrate its tail fast enough to sound like a rattle. They sometimes flatten their heads trying to take on the triangular shape of a rattlesnake's head, but this can be difficult to see when you yourself get into defensive mode.

Just a week earlier, I discovered that a gopher snake, no doubt the same one that surprised me by the clothesline, had shed its skin along the edge of the concrete porch. It left behind an entire intact tube of supple snakeskin, complete with eyes and open mouth. The snakeskin was weightless in my hand, cool and slightly damp, unexpectedly luscious. Unlike a tanned hide from a dead snake—the kind used for belts and boots—a shed skin dries quickly when exposed to the elements and within minutes becomes so fragile it can be torn by a breath. For a week or two, the snake wears two coats at once, until built-up fluids and enzymes allow the old outer layer to separate from its fresh, clean body. The snake then shimmies out of the tight sheath that no longer fits, which stretches slightly as it peels off. If I had come across the snake minutes earlier, I would have discovered not a scary serpent, but a creature made vulnerable by allowing itself to grow.

Ecdysis. The process of shedding one's skin in one continuous layer. Several times a year, a snake grows a new layer of keratinous scales under the old layer, which turns opaque. Each layer of shed skin leaves behind another segment in a rattlesnake's rattle. The number of segments won't tell you how old a snake is, however, because snakes shed their skins at different rates as they age, and rattles can get broken off. But I doubt you want to get close enough to count them, anyway.

I was hanging the last of the newly rinsed laundry when the frenzied birds in the yard began to screech and feint. Their reliable warning system always signaled snake. A three-foot Mohave rattlesnake was winding its way from behind a mesquite tree about forty feet from where I stood. A bite from a Mohave is ten times deadlier than a bite from a western diamondback because it has two types of venom. When you're bitten by a Mohave, you're first attacked by a neurotoxin that paralyzes you before the second hemotoxic venom kicks in. Western diamondbacks, on the other hand, have only the single hemotoxin that destroys blood cells and tissues. A woman in Horseshoe Canyon once stepped on a western diamondback in her yard late at night. She had lived in the Chiricahua Mountains for twenty years and knew better than to walk at night in sandals, but probably thought *Just this once* and *I'm not going far*. No moon lit her way; the nearest streetlight was the one in Rodeo, New Mexico, eight miles away. After hours of throbbing pain, she took an expensive helicopter ride from an emergency room in Douglas to a hospital in Tucson. The next time I saw her was at a community potluck to introduce three new Border Patrol agents. She walked on crutches with one foot wrapped in bandages; on her other foot she wore a sturdy new work boot. She said the experience was a lesson in being present and moving with awareness. She carried no malice toward the snake; rather, she said, her connection with the desert would only deepen as her foot healed. My lesson was to always wear sturdy work boots and carry a brighter flashlight.

When I spotted the Mohave, I reached for the tongs again before I realized I had reached the limits of my courage. Instead I called Barney, a retired herpetologist in Cave Creek Canyon, who was doing research on the relocation of "nuisance rattlesnakes." After years of moving snakes from harm's way, Barney's findings showed that a rattlesnake knew its home range intimately and seldom left its self-imposed boundaries, unless forced.

"Do you think I can somehow corner the snake and keep it from running away until you can get here?" I asked, sounding braver than I felt. "Don't worry," Barney replied. "I'm on my way."

Mercifully, Barney arrived within fifteen minutes and the snake hadn't moved far. Using his extra-long, heavy-gauge metal tongs, he deftly caught the snake and loaded it into a thermal lunch box. Barney thanked me for my donation to his research and waved as he drove off with the rattlesnake sitting beside him on the front seat of his pickup.

According to Barney, rattlesnakes frequent the same hunting and hibernation sites year after year. It used to be thought that if a snake is removed far outside its usual home range, it would wander erratically, exposing itself to predators and other dangers, trying to find its way back home. Old school science presumed that any snakes relocated far from home would die within a year, unable to adapt to their new environment. New technology with surgically implanted radio transmitters offers new data to show that most snakes will either find their way home, if not moved too far, or will settle into their new surroundings. It's as if snakes determine their value of home by weighing the price of safety against the pull of familiarity.

Keratin. A rattlesnake's tail is made of hollow, interlocking segments of keratin that the snake can shake up to ninety times a second. The rattle is designed to send a danger signal to intruders, persuading them to stay away. A rattlesnake would rather scare you than bite you. It costs a rattlesnake significant energy to strike—energy it would prefer to expend on more important things, like catching a meal in a drought-stricken landscape.

In her memoir *The Turquoise Ledge*, Leslie Marmon Silko writes of the rattlesnakes that lived under her furniture. Raised at Laguna Pueblo in New Mexico, she believes a snake is a messenger from the underworld, carrying communication back and forth. The message a snake brings, she writes, is to prepare for change. Snakes don't care whether I am a believer or not; they carry the power of their message regardless.

Brilles. Transparent scales snakes have instead of eyelids to cover their eyes. Snakes can't blink; they sleep with their eyes open, giving the appearance that they are ever-vigilant. When a snake sheds its skin, it sheds the brilles (referred to as "eye caps" or "eye shields" by herpetologists) as well.

Silko wrote that it is possible to be a friend of snakes, that the rattlesnakes that lived under her house in Tucson learned her and her dogs' routines. She said they understood that she meant them no harm. In return for her acceptance, arrowheads and pieces of turquoise began to appear as gifts on her doorstep. Some say that not until we become truly frightened are we able to take steps toward change. Is that a gift from our fear? Here in the landscape of snakes, I welcomed their messages.

Decline. Snakes in Arizona are in a slow but steady decline. Drought, fires, and habitat loss contribute to smaller population numbers and reduced movement in an already narrow range. Poaching also contributes to their decline; rattlesnakes can fetch hundreds of dollars on the black market, despite the fact that they don't make very good pets.

I left my house at noon, aware that the races wouldn't start until the heat of the day had faded. I drove the five miles down Sulphur Canyon Road across the Arizona state line, then passed the turnoff to Cave Creek Canyon and headed east into the New Mexico bootheel. Around

Hachita I aimed south through the Playas Valley on the eastern slope
of the Animas Mountains. The road stretched flat and straight, dipping
into an occasional dry wash. Signs that once commanded "Watch for
water" had been edited with spray paint to implore passersby to "Pray
for rain." A mosaic of sotol, agave, and century plants bristled among
the lovegrass and snakeweed. Irrigated fields dotted the base of a ridge;
a small herd of pronghorn grazed in the distance. The asphalt road
sang a monotone under the tires of my SUV. First one then another
live western diamondback watched me from the verge as I passed; a
mile further lay a dead one, smashed by a pickup truck and pecked at
by turkey vultures.

People go out of their way to drive over snakes and take special
delight in running over rattlers. But even a dead rattlesnake is dangerous;
because of its slow-to-respond nervous system, a snake can bite for a
full hour after its head has been severed from its body. Rattlesnakes are
not aggressive, but will strike if kicked, kissed, or poked with a stick.
In the United States, eight thousand people are bitten every year by
venomous snakes. Most of the victims are drunk at the time.

*Ridge-nosed rattlesnake. The only U.S. rattlesnake species listed as
endangered by the U.S. Fish and Wildlife Service; a subspecies, the Arizona
ridge-nosed, is protected in Arizona. It lives in mountain ranges in southern
Arizona and New Mexico. Another subspecies, the New Mexico ridge-
nosed, is found only at the bottom of Indian Creek Canyon near Animas
Peak. Biologists searched for the snake in this remote canyon in 1974 but
after several months found only eleven individuals. Indian Creek Canyon
is so remote and rugged there are no plans to update the survey.*

As the odometer ticked off another mile, the mesquite grew further apart,
exposing bare rock and sand. Greens and blues went missing; distant

peaks appeared burnt and raw. The colors of the landscape seemed pulled from a single tube of sienna, the pigment of prehistoric cave art. The way I drove morphed, too. Instead of staring through my windshield, intent on my destination, I slowed down, swiveling my neck and marveling at the landscape. I slowed to a crawl as another dead diamondback paralleled the edge of the pavement. Grateful for the lack of traffic, I wished for a bumper sticker that read "I brake for snakes."

Thirty minutes later I arrived in Antelope Wells, the smallest and least-used U.S. border crossing into Mexico. Population two, its only inhabitants were Customs and Border Protection personnel, who lived in trailers behind the crossing station. A uniformed agent waved me through. On the Mexican side, federales with automatic rifles stopped me to ask where I was going. I explained in Spanish that I was there for the horse race and their side looked like more fun. "*Quiero ir a la fiesta*," I said, looking past them for the party. On the American side, ranchers backed their pickups perpendicular to the fence and sat on their tailgates, boots dangling over the edge, to watch the races. On the Mexican side, roving musicians worked the crowd while preteens danced to *rancheras* and *corridos* from a boom box on a makeshift stage. Expressionless, the federales allowed me to park.

I wandered through the small crowd of women selling burritos from camping stoves and vendors hawking *cervesas* from coolers. A girl with a single long braid charged me one American dollar for a toasted quesadilla smothered with green chile, wrapped in foil and nestled in a flimsy cardboard bowl. Bottled water was not offered, so I opted for a lukewarm strawberry soda. I stopped to put the bottle between my feet so I could grab my quesadilla with both hands. In front of me paraded a father walking a pony that carried his tiny daughter, whose dark curls tumbled from a red headband with an enormous purple bow. The father passed the lead rope to his young son, who took his turn piloting the pony. Three ranchers leaned on the edge of the wooden stage, comfortable in each other's company. Each man wore clean new jeans, a crisp white shirt with snaps, and neon orange or lemon yellow or lime green snakeskin boots with matching snakeskin belt and hatband. Their summer Stetsons tilted toward each other as they shared stories about the weather, the land, its people.

I envied their apparent easy sense of belonging to this place. After a year of living here, I was growing to love the mountains and the communities that called these mountains home. Neighbors depended on neighbors, but mostly they depended on themselves. Because the closest grocery store was a hundred-mile round trip away, I had learned to appreciate defrosted food. With only one restaurant and no auto repair shops or department stores—and with online purchases routed through the local post office, who handed them off to FedEx, whose delivery schedule was erratic at best—I was shedding my consumerism like an old skin. But with the closest hospital a helicopter ride away and stories of snakebites and other accidents and maladies a common topic of conversation, feelings of vulnerability amassed with doubts about my capacity to remain here, no matter how much I loved these mountains.

I watched a few races and cheered all entries—winners and losers. Between races, a man in khaki work clothes groomed the finish line with a garden rake. Out here on the border, with no photo finishes or instant replays, the only way to call the winner of a close race was from the memories of the witnesses, the impressions in the dirt, the ghosts of what remained.

Ephemeral. Antoine de Saint-Exupéry wrote that ephemeral things are in danger of disappearing. "It is very rarely that a mountain changes its position...The thing that matters to us is the mountain. It does not change."

As I waited for the next race, I was reminded of a book I have read many times. A little prince lands in a desert, surprised at its emptiness. The first living thing he meets is a snake. When the little prince complains that it is lonely in the desert, the snake replies, "It is also lonely among men."

The little prince's snake claimed to solve all riddles. The snake ultimately agreed to return the little prince to his home far away, but only when the little prince was certain he was ready. The little prince had already learned a secret from a fox, who said that what is essential is invisible to the eye. When the little prince realized he was forgetting how to love his planet and the living things on it, he knew the time had come to ask the snake to send him home. The little prince realized that even his mountains could change, and some things—including himself—could disappear.

Drought. According to the National Oceanic and Atmospheric Administration, average temperatures in Arizona and New Mexico have been rising and drought conditions have been growing more severe since 2000. As a result of changing conditions, scientists expect an accelerated rate of species extinction, especially of already-vulnerable species.

A warm wind raised coils of dust from my footsteps as I walked toward a lone shade tree at the end of the track. From the perspective of the finish line, watching horses and riders compete to be seconds faster than their rivals, I felt time standing still under a cloudless sky and a bootheel sun. The future of this annual event never felt threatened—I assumed it would continue as long as there were quarter Horses and local riders with a competitive streak. Traditions are long-lived, I thought—they die hard. I didn't realize they could be extirpated like a species facing the challenges of isolation.

Antelope Wells. A border crossing so remote that the state authority hadn't kept traffic statistics in years. But by 2013, a $12 million port of entry *would replace the orange cones that I had navigated eight years earlier. The old wire fence would be replaced with a metal vehicle barrier inconducive to friendly competitions. The little girl with the dark curls and her brother would become part of a rapidly changing borderland. Their remembrances of pony rides and fiestas along the border would be replaced with new memories created in an age of infrared technology and walls made of steel bollards. A tradition of cross-cultural exchange and cross-border celebrations will have disappeared.*

Shadows lengthening across the finish line signaled it was time to go home. There was no official program, so I had no idea how many more races, if any, remained, but I wanted to leave in time to catch the twilight. There was a small chance the two live western diamondbacks might still be in the spot where I had passed them.

As I drove north from the border, the low western sun reflected a rose light across the valley. The more fiercely I examined the landscape, the more different kinds of borders emerged—between mountain and meadow, scrub and dirt, stranger and neighbor, old and new, present and future.

Then I saw a familiar silhouette—like a walking stick a hiker might have dropped, only significantly different—in the middle of the road. I stopped the car and lowered my window; the sun warmed my arm. The loamy scent of creosote filled the car. No one was behind me—hadn't been for miles—and no one had come from the opposite direction for at least twenty minutes. I kept the motor running and my foot on the brake. The snake stretched its full length across the dotted line running down the center of the two-lane blacktop. Almost four feet long, it was a black-tailed rattlesnake, a species I had only seen in field guides.

I had never been alone before in the middle of the Badlands with a live rattlesnake, especially not close enough to watch it flick its tongue. A snake uses its tongue to gather chemicals from the air and ground, and then transfers those chemicals to an organ in the roof of its mouth where it processes the information. This snake was following a string of new data as it reached across the asphalt, tranquil enough to give me a good look. Its scales sketched a diamond pattern down its back and a dark mask crossed its face. Its blackish tail with a brown rattle at the tip was unlike the striped tail of a Mohave or a western diamondback. Safely inside my vehicle with thousands of pounds of machine between us, I looked into the snake's unblinking eyes. I thought again of Silko's belief that friendship with snakes is possible.

The black-tail was in no hurry to go anywhere. Older and wiser snakes move away from danger without striking out; younger snakes are more dangerous because they're unpredictable. Some herpetologists believe rattlesnakes rattle their tails not to warn off anything that comes too close, but that they shake from fear, the way most humans do in similar situations. Neither of us felt threatened, although a snake warmed by the sun can quickly recoil and strike if it wants to. The length of its rattle spoke of several years in this valley, but it was clearly unwise to the dangers of the road.

Hibernaculum. Winter home for snakes. Rattlesnakes are solitary animals that nevertheless spend the winter in communal dens, sometimes in large groups, and return each autumn to the same hibernaculum. A young rattlesnake stays with its mother until its first molt at one or two weeks, when it develops its first rattle and can defend itself. The young snake then leaves the den in the spring to forage and in fall follows adult scent trails back to the hibernaculum.

In the quiet of the empty highway, I listened for whatever message the day's snakes were trying to send to me. If the snakes were warning me to prepare for change, I had more questions than answers. How can we solve the riddle of learning to respect our home, the planet, and the living things on it while watching its destruction at our own hands? Is it possible to shed our habits, like skins that no longer fit, of ignoring the essential things we can't see? If extreme events bring about huge changes, what changes will humans be forced to make as temperatures soar, sea levels rise, and climate extremes become commonplace? And if we don't change until we're truly frightened, how much more convincing do we need?

A Swainson's hawk was hunting low above the road. The hawk was considering the black-tailed rattlesnake for a meal and would have nabbed it if I hadn't been so close. Flocks of Swainson's hawks fly south through the New Mexico bootheel during migration season. Large groups of Swainson's hawks sometimes gathered in newly mowed alfalfa fields where Sulphur Canyon Road met State Line Road, where pocket mice and ground squirrels were easy prey. I watched this hawk slowly gain altitude, catching a thermal. So effortless, so at home.

Slate-gray rain clouds swelled on the horizon. When I looked back at the pavement, the snake was gone. I eased my foot off the brake.

What Bluebirds Taught Me About Motherhood

The red coachwhip wound around the black locust tree, its head inches from the entrance to the bluebird box. At almost five feet long, the snake had climbed fully off the ground, its neck arched to poke into the hole. Inside, two nestlings peeped.

I had been watching the birdhouse outside my bedroom window for months. Western bluebirds overwinter in Santa Fe, where I have been living now for several years, and some cold winter mornings I watched four or five males, females, and juveniles pile out of the box like clowns out of a Volkswagen after spending the night huddled together for warmth. In April the antics of the eager male, quivering his wings and gamboling on the branches of the locust tree to the amusement of the judgmental female, greeted me most mornings. By early May the new couple shot into the entrance hole of the birdhouse with remarkable precision, carrying building materials of twigs, grasses, and feathers. While the eggs lay in the nest, warm and cozy underneath mom, dad brought a caddis fly or lacewing home for dinner. I first heard the tiny voices around Memorial Day. By then both adults hunted nearby, carrying insects to feed the hatchlings with increasing intensity.

I enjoyed watching this little scene of domesticity, perhaps because it was so entirely missing from my life. I fall into the census category of "childless," a disagreeable term that defines a woman not by what she is but by what she doesn't have. The definition of the term skirts the issue of whether a woman finds herself in this state as a result of choice, biology, economics, philosophy, or simple procrastination. Except nothing about reproduction and its aftermath is ever simple.

Bluebirds are quiet birds, but the bright June morning the snake appeared, both parents complained loudly enough to catch my attention even as I sat at my computer on the other side of the house. The birds flitted around the snake but weren't big and mean enough to actually attack it. And yet they made their intention clear.

Let's take a minute to contrast the beauty of the bluebird and the menace of the coachwhip. An ancient battle fraught with symbolism was being fought in my high desert garden. In Navajo culture a bluebird is an allegory of creativity and creation, but a snake communicates with the supernatural. In Christian religions the snake is blamed for the mess we've inherited, all because of a woman's desire for more. I maintain a healthy respect for snakes and find them fascinating, beautiful, and maligned. On the other hand, I am an active advocate for bluebirds—I clean out the nest box each fall, put out dried mealworms in spring, and toss pillows at menacing scrub jays during nesting season. But I was being tested in my own little Eden. Contestants on an ancient battlefield were about to collide, and my sympathies were being called out. Even inaction counts as action, especially regarding life and death in a nest box.

I grabbed a garden hose and blasted the snake. Startled, it slid up the branches of the locust tree until both it and I realized it could either return down the path that it had taken or fall on my head. The coachwhip was smart enough to choose the first option and spiraled back to the nest box. I continued my offensive, nervous that the snake would try again to get inside the box, if only to get away from me. I also worried about how to spray the box without getting its contents wet. I had a split second to balance defending the babies against possibly soaking them. When the snake wound its way around the box again, I inadvertently soaked the box.

As I pressed my thumb harder over the end of the hose, I tried to justify my choice. I was only doing what every other privileged human has been doing on the planet for millennia—playing God, deciding who deserves to live and who should go hungry, my choices propped up by rational arguments about declining species numbers and subjective aesthetics. But my logic was skewed. What did I know of the conservation status of red coachwhips in the desert southwest? (IUCN: Adult population size unknown, current population trend stable.) By denying the snake its meal, was I taking charge of my environment out of habit, out of control, or because it felt good? Was I just another example of everything out of whack in the world?

The answer depends on who is looking. Consider the constant noise about the sanctity of motherhood, its undisputed joys, and the argument in this country over whether women should even be given that choice. When I was growing up on the South Side of Chicago, all the women I knew were either mothers or nuns. Neither role appealed to me, precisely because they seemed to be my only two choices. Except for the two weeks in grade school when I tried to hedge my bets about my "calling" and attended after-school vocation classes led by Sister John Kathleen, joining the convent was as unpleasant to me as childbirth. If an aunt or cousin handed me a baby to hold, I would develop a sudden need to do something—anything—else. I belong to the 40 percent of American women who have never given birth. I never tried to feed an ailing infant or keep an altricial newborn safe. I am proof that motherhood does not come naturally to all women. In fact, when birth control failed, twice, I terminated not one but two pregnancies—decisions not easily made at the time but about which I have no regrets. I am not alone in this sentiment.

The coachwhip hit the ground and raced toward the back gate, where I assumed it had slipped out of the courtyard. But ten minutes later the snake's red head peered like a periscope over the rock steps leading down to the gate. A second male bluebird, part of an extended family group from what I assumed was the previous year's brood, joined me and the parents, who were still perched in the tree, noisily defending the nest. Together, aided by the garden hose, we made the snake feel unwelcome, our vigil lasting more than an hour. After repeatedly sticking its neck above the rocks only to be shot in the head with a hot stream of water, the snake finally disappeared.

Determined to be sure the birds and I were rid of the threat, I called a neighbor, who showed up with snake tongs fashioned from a long-handled hedge trimmer, packing foam, and duct tape. We disassembled the rock steps that led to the gate but found no trace of the snake. I spread a band of rock salt around its pathway for good measure. I have no idea where I got the idea that rock salt could be an effective barrier of any kind—it isn't. It served only as a measure of my desperation and helplessness. It also underscored where my loyalties lay, although in the heat of the battle I never once questioned my aversion to the snake. Perhaps because, unlike my bluebird box watch, I had never witnessed the snake family's struggles to survive and had never met its cute little snakelets. Or maybe because snakes have never in popular white American culture been associated with happiness, but rather the opposite. Coachwhips have an undeserved reputation for aggression, when they actually dislike humans as much as we dislike them, and can race away at speeds up to eight miles an hour. Despite their unfortunate name, they will not whip you to death with their tails, although they will jump at your face if cornered. They find rodents, lizards, and other snakes as tasty as birds, and I knew the snake could easily find a snack in the green space on the other side of my courtyard wall. As my neighbor and I reassembled the rock steps to the back gate, I trusted the snake to remain gone. I felt satisfied as the guardian of my garden.

Around lunchtime a warm breeze picked up, which I hoped the coachwhip would find annoying. I peeked at the box through a window, surprised to see one of the nestlings sticking his head as far as he could outside the entrance hole. He was straining so hard his tiny claws were gripping the edge of the hole. Within seconds he had gotten his body wedged into the opening until he suddenly popped out and onto the horizontal branch that stretched in front of the box. The wind had grown stronger, and the nestling clutched at the branch, tottering front and back like a drunken sailor on high seas. He soon lost the fight against the force that would one day sustain him, as a wind he couldn't negotiate blew him off the branch. I now had one fledgling on the ground, one nestling still in the box, and a hungry snake on the prowl.

The fledgling displayed amazingly astute survival skills—staying almost invisible from the neighborhood hawks and owls; emerging from hiding places behind lilac bushes and tall grasses just long enough to beg for food; confidently leaping onto rock walls when one of his parents arrived with lunch. He grew stronger. No snake appeared. One morning after he had spent three days on the ground, I found him standing in the middle of a round patio table. He seemed as perplexed as I was about how he had gotten there and what to do next. Maybe he was contemplating the awesomeness of aerodynamics. Maybe he was astounded by his new freedom. Or perhaps he was preparing for the huge leap he was about to make. We looked at each other for several long seconds before he flew, full of grace, to the low branches of a nearby peach tree.

Outside the courtyard wall the parents had already begun building a new nest in a second nest box. This box sat atop a wooden post designed to deter a climbing snake. I'm sure the parents intended this box to remain unmolested by scrub jays and coachwhips, but I wondered what else they were planning. Ornithologists say that to the parents the value of a brood is directly proportional to the cost of replacing it.

This little family had already experienced significant loss. About a week before the first nestling fledged, I watched the female struggling inside the nest box, pulling and tugging at something obviously heavy. After wresting it free, she pushed it through the entrance hole and carried it off. I knew it was a newly hatched bluebird, but I didn't know if it was alive or dead or dying. She landed in a juniper tree on the other side of the courtyard wall, minus the baby. I traced her flight path, fruitlessly searching the ground and the heavens to understand what had happened. Did the baby die after hatching? What killed it? Maybe it was still alive. Why would a mother carry off a living baby? Were they moving to the other nest box? Had they been disturbed? Was I to blame? The next day I watched the male do the same thing, but this time I found what he dropped. The baby bird, eyes closed and naked except for a few wisps of what looked like hair and the beginnings of pinfeathers on wings smaller than its head, lay under a lilac bush. It showed no signs of injury or attack. Its translucent skin revealed an abdomen swollen with the yolk it had swallowed before hatching. It was crusty, tragic, and dead.

Biologists had been saying that with the drought New Mexico was experiencing in 2013, only 25 to 30 percent of fledglings would survive compared to about 50 percent in ideal circumstances, and 90 to 95 percent of the birds that did survive after fledging would die before they were old enough to reproduce. This added up to mean that only 22.5 birds out of a hundred would make it past their first year. Of the four eggs laid in my nest box, two babies died before fledging, one had successfully navigated its way to the peach tree, and one remained an unknown in the box. Four days had passed, but the second nestling hadn't left home. The parents still came to the nest box bringing dinner, which Bluebird Baby #2 willingly ate, but it was evidently less eager to follow its sibling out into the world. I wondered if my spray had indeed prompted Bluebird Baby #1 to jump too soon. The strong, confident behavior he displayed outside in the courtyard gave me hope he would survive, although to my knowledge, I never saw him or the snake again.

On the fifth day after the first bluebird fledged, Bluebird Baby #2 popped out of the nest box, miscalculated the horizontal branch, and tumbled to the ground. She immediately displayed a personality different from Bluebird Baby #1. She seemed hesitant, alone, and afraid. She stumbled when she tried to hop up a step. She didn't hide under the lilac bushes but remained out in the open and cried nonstop. Dad with a bug in his beak appeared on the courtyard wall only once, watched the baby cry and beg, and flew off, still gripping the bug. Mom only occasionally glanced baby's way while continuing to build the new nest in the box beyond the wall.

I listened to the baby bluebird cry for two days, unanswered, as it begged for food. The more it cried, the angrier I grew. My anger had its own evolution. At first I couldn't understand all the work the parents had put into this little family only to give up on a life barely begun. I found it hard to accept that the mother had made a commitment to lay the eggs and incubate them for two weeks; both parents hunted for food and defended against predators, only to stop short of giving each fledgling all the energy, attention, and resources they could afford. My anger was critical and accusing and growing as I watched the mother busily building the new nest fifty yards away and showing no interest in the life already here now. I began to doubt the infallibility of the instincts that drive birds and animals through the patterns of their days. "Hey!" I shouted at the mother once as she flew to the other nest box. "Somebody's hungry over here!"

But what did I know about being a mother? By my reckoning, maternal instincts are not innate. When, as a teenager, I tried to envision my life as an adult, I never saw kids in the picture. I adore puppies and kittens but feel no connection to newborn humans. Although I have always smiled and pretended to admire babies and pregnant women, I figure that the planet is already about to collapse from the burden of carrying us all. I don't need to contribute to that weight.

I was watering the hollyhocks early the third morning when I spotted her. A fuzz ball of spotted down and pinfeathers, Bluebird Baby #2 was standing with her head tucked under her wing, next to a bush less than ten feet from me. I was so startled I spoke to her.

"There you are," I said, surprised that she made no attempt to move away. At seven o'clock in the morning the June sun had been baking the ground for an hour. The fledgling had not taken refuge from the heat or the predators. But at the sound of my voice she picked up her head and looked at me with an expression of absolute sorrow. I moved slightly closer. "Are you okay?" I asked.

She tried to move and tipped over. With barely the energy to spread one wing to break her fall, she opened her beak and began to pant.

She lay not far from the locust tree. Her nest box now sat quiet and empty. She had only been out of her shell for maybe three weeks; she had only been out of the nest box and on the ground for two days. As I saw it, those two days were the most forlorn, cruel, and empty days.

I put down my watering can and sat on the ground in front of the bird. There was nothing I could do but bear witness to her existence, even as it ended. "I'm so sorry," I said. We sat together in the sun for twenty minutes, until the bird collapsed and breathed its last breath, and I went back into the house.

When I tell friends the story of the bluebird, they ask me questions I can't answer. Why didn't you save it? Why didn't you pick it up and put it in a box and bring it to the Wildlife Rehabilitation Center? Why didn't you do something—anything?

The convenient truth is it never entered my mind. I was so busy being indignant at the mother's behavior, I never considered intervening. I can make excuses—I had other things to do, I was busy working, I wasn't always home. I had no idea how to care for an abandoned fledgling. The Norwegian writer Karl Ove Knausgaard has written, "Indifference is one of the seven deadly sins, actually the greatest of them all, because it is the only one that sins against life." Was I indifferent? Was this mother? Were we both sinners?

I needed answers. I called the Cornell Lab of Ornithology and spoke to a woman named Robin. Why did this have to happen? Had a virus infected the nest box? That explanation was plausible in New Mexico and could account for the deaths of the first two birds that hadn't fledged. Perhaps Bluebird Baby #1 was resilient enough with a strong-enough immune system to flourish in spite of the virus, but Bluebird Baby #2 was just less fortunate, gene-wise. Was something else wrong with Bluebird Baby #2 that I couldn't see? Maybe I had damaged Bluebird Baby #2 with my blast from the hose. Maybe she never would have made it anyway. Or maybe this scenario was playing out according to rules I would never be privy to.

Robin explained that parents need to balance the demands of their fledglings against the maintenance of themselves and the species. In purely biological terms, the parents make an investment in the future. Increasing one baby's chance of survival—the ultimate goal being, of course, reproductive success—comes at the cost of investment in other offspring. But, I asked Robin, how do the parents do that math? At what point are the parents giving more than they can afford?

The parents analyze their offspring and rely on cues to determine the chances their babies have of being successful, Robin explained. Mathematical models suggest that parents allocate more resources to bigger, stronger, and more colorful babies when resources are scarce. I argued that I had enough mealworms in feeders to keep the entire family sated for weeks, and there seemed to be no dent in the lacewing population. I craved answers that Robin didn't have. Did the mother stop feeding Bluebird Baby #2 because she knew it was going to die? Or did it die because she stopped feeding it?

The calculation that a female bluebird must make is simple. Her single-minded goal is the success of future generations; her vision reaches beyond herself. I once mentioned to a friend—another childless woman—that one day I might regret not having children, because who would care for me in my doddering old age? That's a lousy reason to have a kid, she replied.

Terry Tempest Williams has written that to become a mother is an unspoken agreement to be forever vulnerable. A thesaurus tells me that the opposite of vulnerable is impregnable. I know that I am neither. My math is also simple—I am the sum of my decisions, only one of which was to not have children. A selfish decision, maybe, that was actually made out of generosity. I knew at a young age that I wanted a career; when I got older, I didn't have the resources to help me juggle both a career and a child. It would be unfair to the children, I felt, if I couldn't give them the care and devotion they deserved. I know my choice is not the choice another woman might make, but it was and still is right for me.

Like the snake in the garden that tempted the first woman to make a decision, my coachwhip taught me that every decision has consequences that live for generations. I am certain that the bluebird mother would agree. Even my decision not to have children has consequences that will live beyond me; I am reminded of this as I work through the genealogy in my family tree.

A month later, the second and last brood of the summer hatched in the nest box outside the courtyard wall and survived fledging with no help from me. This fall I will once again clean out the nest box; I will continue to refresh the water in the birdbath and replenish the mealworms in the feeders daily. It is the least I can do to make up for the damaging impact I have had on their habitat. A vision that reaches beyond any individual starts with the individual. We all find success in our own ways.

What the Two Percent Are Saying

I didn't see a single prairie dog. I scanned a landscape dotted with piñon and juniper; I could spot bare patches among the rabbit brush and grama grasses. The dirt berms that circled the burrow entrances were obvious, but the only things moving were ravens, my companion, and me.

A volunteer involved with prairie dog relocation had brought me here, to an alluvial plain downstream from an escarpment along the Rio Grande. She was careful to protect the secrecy of the spot; I signed a confidentiality agreement before I got out of her truck and promised not to divulge the location under any circumstances. So we may or may not have been in the Rio Grande Valley, and maybe I just like the sound of the words *escarpment* and *alluvial plain*. A team of volunteers had moved almost five hundred Gunnison's prairie dogs away from the path of development around Albuquerque and Santa Fe; the group was invested in the animals' survival and their future in northern New Mexico. Considered by ranchers, horse owners, and weekend gardeners to be the vermin of the American Southwest, prairie dogs are killed more often than rescued. Gunnison's prairie dogs, which were once abundant across northern New Mexico and southern Colorado, have declined by ninety-eight percent in the last one hundred years; the other four species of prairie dogs have experienced similar declines. Texas once claimed the largest prairie dog town, covering twenty-five thousand square miles and hosting four hundred million prairie dogs. But that was in 1901.

A rodent in the same family as chipmunks and marmots, a prairie dog is a pear-shaped bundle of fur and fleas with a short, straight tail. It can stand on its hind legs and hold food in its front paws, which are shaped like an old man's hands. Black-tailed prairie dogs were first described by Meriwether Lewis in 1804 during the Lewis and Clark Expedition across South Dakota; he called them *barking squirrels*. Its genus, Cynomys, comes from the Greek word for *dog mouse*. They are also known as *yaprats, petit chiens*, and *sod poodles*.

As my companion and I approached the relocation site, three sentinel prairie dogs popped out of their burrows on the other side of an arroyo. The three formed a wide triangle, guarding the edges of their territory. Their alarm calls, faint at a distance, sounded like a cross between a northern flicker's caw and a Chihuahua's bark, notifying their community they had guests. No other prairie dogs showed themselves, however, and eventually even the sentinels returned down under. I wondered what was happening underground, hidden and mysterious to creatures like me who didn't speak their language.

Studies have shown that prairie dogs have one of the largest vocabularies in the animal kingdom, with more sophisticated language skills than whales, dolphins, or parrots. Prairie dogs have different calls for *hawk, coyote, dog,* and *rattlesnake.* They have a call for *human* and can add syllables to that call to say *tall human in a blue shirt* and *thin human in a white shirt* and *short, fat human in a yellow shirt.* A prairie dog in Utah can invent a new call for something she has never seen before, and a prairie dog in Colorado will understand what that call means the first time he hears it. Prairie dogs do not need dictionaries.

Prairie dog alarm calls convey information about the speed at which a predator is approaching and from what distance. This information is essential to their survival; they run for cover faster if a low-flying hawk is diving than if a coyote on a ridge line is trotting. I could only imagine what the sentinels were saying about the two women hiking toward them, one carrying a bucket of sunflower seeds, the other perhaps recognizable to them. I hoped they had a word for *friend*.

Research has deciphered about a hundred prairie dog words, which doesn't indicate the limits to their vocabulary—it only indicates the limits of the research. Words not discovered include, for example, the prairie dog words for housing developments, bulldozers that level their towns, or the concrete that plugs what were once their homes. Nor is it known if prairie dogs have a word for the plague that decimates populations across the American West. Although New Mexico reports more than half the human cases of bubonic plague in the United States, fewer than three percent of those infections were transmitted through prairie dogs or their fleas, according to the Centers for Disease Control.

The federal government has spent tens of millions of dollars poisoning prairie dogs, and state and local governments do the same. In late 2013, the Thunder Basin National Grassland in Wyoming announced a plan to poison or shoot sixteen thousand prairie dogs within park boundaries. In South Dakota and Wyoming, landowners are required by law to poison prairie dogs living on their property. Fines for noncompliance range from fifty dollars to twenty-five hundred dollars a day.

One style of prairie dog hunting is known as "whack 'em and stack 'em." Hunters hang push-button counters on lanyards around their necks to track their body count. The Red Mist Society delights in watching the impact on prairie dogs from their exploding dum-dum bullets. In parts of New Mexico, hunters refer to prairie dogs as *tails,* because that is often the only body part remaining. A gun shop in Los Lunas, New Mexico held a contest in 2013; the shooter who collected the most tails won a semi-automatic rifle. The final tally of the weeklong competition was fifteen hundred tails; the winner bagged two hundred and thirty-nine.

Research has shown that prairie dogs have a call for a person who has fired a shotgun, and that it's different from the call they used for the same person before he fired the gun. I want to add that word to my vocabulary and try it out on friends in Utah and Colorado and see if they know what I mean. Prairie dogs continue to use the new name for that shooter for up to two months, whether or not he carries a gun. This tells me that prairie dogs have memories, but the more interesting consideration is whether the call implies the degree of danger that the person with the shotgun poses, or whether the prairie dog is expressing a different sentiment. Outrage? vengeance? or simple disgust?

My companion had been monitoring the health and success rates of the prairie dogs in their new burrows for the last five years. We were out in late October, past the start of prairie dog hibernation time. She said that the animals reach a body weight that triggers a chemical in their blood, signaling when to tunnel into the warm earth to live off stored fat. From October until May, they inhabit the underworld, in tunnels up to fifty feet long by six inches wide, sleeping close together in small, dark rooms. As we walked across the field, we saw no more prairie dogs, not even the sentinels. We did find fresh scat, which told us the burrows were still active. I tossed handfuls of sunflower seeds down the openings, hoping an alert prairie dog would wake from a seasonal torpor long enough to find lunch. I imagined the landscape in the spring when the ground is green with sun sedges and broadleaf forbs, and prairie dog calls ring across the valley. I tried to imagine what they dreamed about all winter, and if they prayed for rain.

In North America, prairie dogs are a keystone species, which means they make the world a better place without even trying. Keystone species are named for the stone at the apex of an arch. Like an arch without its keystone, an ecosystem can collapse if a keystone species disappears. Despite the poverty of their numbers, just the presence of prairie dogs makes the environment richer and benefits hundreds of other species. Prairie dog burrows help channel rainwater back into the water table, preventing runoff and erosion. Prairie dogs aerate the soil across grasslands and can even reverse the soil compaction that results from cattle grazing. Their foraging forces new grasses to grow. In turn, the fresh grasses offer more nutrients for large herbivores like bison, pronghorn, and deer, who prefer to graze on land that they have shared with prairie dogs. Their gifts to us might not be as immediately recognizable as a welcoming entrance hole to a burrowing owl, or lunch for a black-footed ferret. Life depends on prairie dogs in symbiotic relationships not quite understood.

Prairie dogs live in communities of loosely formed families called *coteries*. They greet each other by approaching slowly and then pressing their mouths together in a gesture called a *greet-kiss*. Biologists who study prairie dogs don't know why the animals do this but have posited various theories—that they get information about the type of food the other prairie dog has eaten, or they identify individuals, or they set hierarchies within the coterie. All these theories have been invalidated by observation over time. What has been shown, however, is that a greet-kiss between males from different territories leads to a madcap chase, although rarely physical combat. A greet-kiss between females results in a foraging party.

My guess about a greet-kiss is based on my vision of life in the middle of a fourteen-foot tunnel. It's hard to know who you're bumping into in the dark. I can think of no better way than a greet-kiss to establish identity, mine or other tunnel navigators. Identifying another individual in the dark means knowing who you are, who your cousins are, and who your enemies are. By defining ourselves, we define the other, and we can choose to let that definition separate or unite. The ability to self-identify, like language, is an attribute historically awarded only to humans. The thought that we are not separate from animals is a hard realization for many people to embrace. What's left that makes us human—desire? ambition? or the ability to screw things up on a global scale?

Prairie dogs solve the challenge of changing direction in a dark, confining burrow by carving out side chambers called *turnarounds*, small enough to just accommodate an animal who has changed course. Scientists have gleaned few facts from the underground lives of prairie dogs; they are often the first to admit that the more they learn, the more they realize they don't know. When I was a young girl, I believed heaven was whatever I wanted it to be. My heaven was a place where all of life's mysteries would be revealed and I would finally have some answers. In heaven, I'll know what kind of UFO crashed in Roswell, New Mexico and appreciate quantum physics. But I still won't understand why we allowed prairie dogs to disappear.

A prairie dog alarm call lasts only a tenth of a second. But if you record it, slow it down, and slice it up, you can unpack the information and hear the syllables contained in each call. If you slow it down enough, it starts to sound like the song of a humpback whale. If you speed up a whale song, it starts to sound like human speech, although the noises might seem as indecipherable to human ears as prairie dog calls in real-time. A typical male Gunnison's prairie dog dies before he reaches age five; a humpback whale can live to be fifty years old. What does this tell us about the way these animals experience time, and their sense of urgency? I have already outlived the norm for either species. What message does this promise for me, if I could only listen?

Most Americans live by the clock; time is money. Time flows, like water in an arroyo after a hard rain. We can waste, save, and kill time. The future is budgeted; the past is spent. But not all cultures live by the clock. Some languages have no words for *past* or *future*. Some languages have no verb tenses. Many individuals live outside clock time. Consider the young, the old, or the sick. Maybe it's someone you knew or will know, in the past or future. Maybe you wish it could be you.

For the remaining two percent of the billions of prairie dogs that once called the American Southwest home, the clock is ticking. If they are aware of their future, we see no indication. Perhaps time is solely a human construct; maybe humans are the only ones who are concerned about the future. But I am painting with too broad a brush—some of us are not worried at all, and most of us are not worried enough.

As I carried the empty sunflower seed bucket across the arroyo, I looked over my shoulder, hoping for one last glimpse of a prairie dog. At least I knew the colony was still active, unlike other colonies across the Southwest that have been destroyed in so many ways, whether from plague, development, or eradication. A mourning dove called from the top of a cottonwood. How would my view of the world change if I understood the language of prairie dogs? How would our sense of time and community change if we all understood? Unless we carve out our turnaround, we may never know.

Time Passes like Water

"The thing in the world I am most afraid of is fear...fear is more importunate and insupportable than death itself."

Michel de Montaigne

From where I sit on this flat rock floor, I see no way out. If I lift my face up and to the left, my headlamp illuminates the steep trail that I just clambered down, ducking in the tight spots with low clearance. The path wormholes in such crimped arcs that I can't see the entrance to the cave, ninety feet above. But what I realize now—and couldn't have seen on my way down—is that the path runs along the solid edge of an abyss.

My headlamp provides the only light here in this enormous chamber. The ceiling, if I can call it that, is at least thirty feet high and extends above the abyss. The cave walls are solid limestone; almost no loose gravel litters the ground. When I look to my right and my left, the light from my headlamp hints at one or two side tunnels, but I know they lead only to smaller, deeper chambers. The only way out of this place is to go back the way I came. I'm not ready for that, so I stay where I am. Sitting here, I can finally straighten my back without hitting my head; I can sense how badly my knees are shaking. I'm grateful for this firm rock slab under my crossed legs, in the dead center of this chamber, far from the brink of any underground cliffs, where I feel, at least for the moment, safe.

About twenty feet in front of me, my companions are descending into the deep black hole that is the abyss. I told them I will stay here on this canted floor and wait. I watch five headlamps grow dimmer as they spring confidently from boulder to rock ledge, down passages ever steeper and more narrow. We believe there is a river somewhere at the bottom of this cave; we believe there *is* a bottom to this cave. My companions are determined to come up against a limit they can't transcend, whether a constraint imposed by the massive walls of the cave or by their own physical and emotional abilities. No telling how far they will go, but they have dropped so far down that no glow from their headlamps reaches me now. As the magnitude of what I have gotten myself into sinks in, the thought of going deeper underground only makes my anxiety worse. I have reached my limit; I don't need to test it further.

I turn off my headlamp and close my eyes and listen. Faintly, I hear my companions in some other tunnel talking with the hushed reverence the space invites. Eventually their voices trail off and I am left in a silence so dense it slams against my ears. An occasional drip of water seeps from a centuries-old stalactite still growing over the abyss. I feel as tiny as that drip, infinitesimally small here in the innards of the Earth. My heart pounds so hard I can feel it when I put my hand to my chest.

I realize I'm taking in shallow, staccato breaths. The longer I think about the drop-off on the side of the path out of here, the deeper my panic becomes. I imagine making one wrong move and my foot slipping off that smooth rock. I see myself trying to grab a handhold, my fingertips unable to support my weight. I feel my chest, thighs, head bumping against rock walls as I fall through the abyss, only to land on an inaccessible ledge somewhere with who knows how many things broken. I imagine lying wrecked for hours, maybe days, waiting for someone to fetch ropes to haul me out (if anyone *can* haul me out), praying the batteries in my headlamp don't die.

I can't remember why I thought this was a good idea. It sounded like an adventure back in the dining room of the Southwestern Research

Station in Cave Creek Canyon. The station has served as a base camp for scientists doing field work since 1955, when the American Museum of Natural History purchased a dude ranch in southeastern Arizona with money donated by David Rockefeller. In addition to making it possible for biologists to carry out research projects in the ecologically diverse Chiricahua Mountains, the station also lets hangers-on like me enjoy the quiet at fifty-four hundred feet among rhyolite pinnacles and tuffaceous sky islands. It's the place I return to now that I am no longer a resident here in these mountains. I especially love sitting beneath the sycamores, watching the ebb and flow of hawks and frogs and skunks and stars.

One of the volunteers had suggested it, said he had heard Arizona locals consider Crystal Cave a favorite destination. "People have stolen most of the crystals," Nick said, "but it's still a fascinating place." He and three other staff members at the research station had already set aside the weekend to go exploring. Like the other volunteers, Nick was between jobs/schools, cautiously making decisions that would determine his course in life. Shy and soft-spoken, he had a reputation among his colleagues for an impulsive relationship with the outdoors.

"I heard you got lost once hiking in the canyon," I said. I was standing behind him in the breakfast line, staring at an outline of Mount Rushmore stenciled on the back of his T-shirt. The lack of irony in the drawing made me smile.

Nick stopped spooning scrambled eggs onto his plate and turned to face me. His eyes widened and his eyebrows collided as an ancient ache bloomed slowly across his typically deadpan expression. What I had thought was kind of a joke struck him as not funny at all. "I was camping in the backcountry for five days and got off the trail. I eventually found my way to that park on Highway 80," he said, his voice small and pinched.

I knew the spot—a desolate acre of desert delineated by a chain-link fence. Two bushes and some tumbleweed that had not yet blown away were the only signs of life in the park. Sheet metal roofs provided squares of shade over a smattering of picnic tables. A rusted metal slide in the sun next to a teeter-totter and a jungle gym made from plumbing pipes hinted that this was supposed to be a place to have fun. I had never seen anyone there.

"I waited on one of the picnic tables until someone drove by. I don't remember how long I was there—maybe a few hours. I fell asleep."

I pictured him sleeping soundly on a picnic table—a thirty-year-old guy with faith in his fate. I could see him accepting a ride from a passing rancher, trusting that he would arrive safely at the research station, fifteen miles back up canyon. His passion for experiencing the world was tempered by his willingness to accept what came his way. It was a combination of traits I personally found mutually exclusive. I had decided thirty years ago when I was Nick's age that settling for what life sent my way wasn't enough—my impatience sent me in search of a future that was already on its way. I was eighteen when I first hitchhiked across the country; twenty-two when I rode horseback across the Arizona Strip; twenty-eight when I rafted through miles of whitewater. I wondered if Nick had discovered the difference between complacency and contentment. I wondered if I ever would.

The cook had been listening to the conversation about Crystal Cave and now eyed us skeptically from behind the food counter. "You would never get me in that cave," Vickie said, standing with her hands on her hips, serving spoon angled out. "That's pure crazy." She shook her head and looked straight at me. "Last year a woman about your age tried to hike up to the cave and got so scared just from the trail that she couldn't move. We had to practically carry her back down the mountain. She never even got near the cave."

My first reaction was to scoff at the hiker frozen with fear. Ridiculous, I sneered. How does giving in to helplessness get you anywhere, especially back down a mountain? My second reaction was to bristle at the reference to my age and whatever I presumed it insinuated. I was older than Vickie and probably older than the woman stuck on the side of the mountain, and twice as old as the volunteers planning this adventure into Crystal Cave. What did age have to do with anything?

"Some hiker," I mumbled, scowling into my coffee.

Nick watched me struggle with my decision. "You should come with us," he encouraged. "This is why you're here. You're destined to go caving."

My only cave experience had been with Kartchner Caverns, a state park in southeastern Arizona. I had stopped there on my way to Tucson one March morning years ago. After buying a $23 ticket, I passed through the entrance—two giant locked and pressurized doors engineered to preserve the cavern environment, stabilized at a temperature of 70 degrees with 99 percent humidity. I was immediately misted head to toe with what I hoped was water, the intention being, I guessed, to keep the interior pristine. Once on the main path, visitors walked along a sturdy surface finished with a non-slip coating, guided by hand railings and poured concrete curbs, lit by electric lights that the ranger switched on and off as we passed. The paths were wide enough to accommodate a wheelchair kept handy for anyone who requested one. My ninety-minute experience felt as treacherous as taking a docent tour at an art museum, but with different wall art. The ranger's relentless enthusiasm told me everything I needed to know about stalactites and stalagmites, limestone and speleothems. But it wasn't until I went to Crystal Cave that I learned that Kartchner is a *show* cave. Crystal Cave is a *wild* cave. There is a difference.

The volunteers passed a signup sheet down both sides of the dining room table. The permit released the U.S. Forest Service from liability should any of us get hurt. When it came to me, I read, "Persons signing this permit accept responsibility for informing themselves of the inherent dangers of exploring undeveloped caves, and accept full responsibility for their conduct and personal safety."

Pen in hand, I scanned the table. The voices of the four volunteers on my left grew more excited as they described passages and bottlenecks they wanted to explore, with names like Devil's Elbow and Awesomeness and Fat Man's Misery.

"I can guess why it's called Fat Man's Misery," I said.

"I heard it's so tight you have to wiggle through it for about forty or fifty feet. You can't change your mind after you're inside—you're either on your back or your stomach. It's a commitment," said one of the volunteers.

"I won't have to make that decision, right?" I kept my lips in a straight line, unsure how to hold the corners of my mouth. "Fat Man's Misery is optional?"

"It's so narrow in places you have to turn your head to one side or your nose gets scraped. In another place you have to exhale so you don't get hung up."

I couldn't tell if I really wanted to do this or if I just thought I should. A quote from Franklin Roosevelt began to echo in my head. At his inaugural address, he famously said, "… the only thing we have to fear is fear itself—nameless, unreasoning, unjustified terror, which paralyzes needed efforts to … advance." This was 1932, eleven years after polio paralyzed him from the waist down. He devised ways to disguise his disability, including swiveling his hips with the help of crutches to give the appearance of walking. FDR was elected governor of New York in 1929 and president of the United States in 1932, the only person with disabilities ever elected to either position. I imagined him summoning the courage to play a part that no longer fit him and wondered how much it cost him. Did he let his carefully crafted public persona overwrite his own personal image? Was he honest with himself about what he could and couldn't do or did he lose sight of his truth? In his push to pass for something he was not, could he recognize himself when he looked in the mirror?

Steve, who was sitting on my right, had been inside Crystal Cave before. He returned to the research station every summer to work on maintenance projects after months of traveling and visiting family.

"I never found the river, but I can show you what I know." He sipped his coffee and glanced my way. "It's not that bad. And I don't intend to stay down very long. We could leave whenever you're ready."

His faded flannel shirt and work boots gave him the air of a lumberjack; his leather-backed hands, wiry torso, and close-cropped gray hair evidenced a long lifetime spent working outside. He was the only person at the table even remotely my age.

"It might even be fun," he said, still looking at me. When he smiled the lines deepened down the sides of his face, traces of an old habit.

I smiled back and signed my name above the sentence, "The Federal Government assumes no responsibility for any mental or physical injury or damages resulting from entering or exploring the above cave."

Just to be clear, I'm not afraid of heights, nor am I claustrophobic. I'm not even afraid of the dark. But inside this twisted underground I am enveloped in an expansive atmospherelessness. I am neither hot nor cold, wet nor dry; I smell nothing. With my headlamp still off, I open my eyes but my vision doesn't adjust; the blackness is absolute. I am presently so far from light I am reminded of Chiricahua night skies, where the heavens are perforated with history disguised as starlight. I am removed even from my own past.

In my twenties and thirties, still learning what I was capable of, I often muddled through tight spots alone, too proud or ashamed to ask for help. Sometimes it worked, like the time I took off my skis and walked down a Taos mountainside behind my friends rather than admit I didn't know how to ski or ask someone to teach me. Or the day I spent hours lost in Budapest. I found my way back to my hotel without stopping once to ask for directions. I refused to admit I couldn't find my way and didn't speak Hungarian.

The passage of time like the passage of water reforms what was once undeniably solid. The river that carved this cave exploited the vulnerability of its limestone walls. The empty places are oblivious to the rock's former resistance; the water leaves behind only the memory of what has been diminished.

I turn my headlamp back on. Its weak beam casts shadows on a far wall. A calmer, more sensible version of myself might have remembered what Plato wrote about caves. "The bewilderments of the eyes are of two kinds, and arise from two causes, either from coming out of the light or from going into the light." The shadows in Plato's cave were only a projection of one version of reality, cast to convince those stuck in the cave to seek the truth, to find what is real. My truth, here in Crystal Cave, is already real. I too am stuck, at the limits of my ability in this moment.

I close my eyes again. Sometimes the best way to see something is to stop staring at it. Steve has promised to return so I won't have to navigate my exit alone, but I wasn't counting on needing much more than a companion. Trying to climb back up that precarious path without help, now that I am aware of the precipice, means facing a fear as intense as this space is profound. Asking for assistance means admitting I'm not the self-sufficient, invincible woman I believe myself to be. I can't decide which choice is easier.

Is this how it begins—asking for help for something I once could do alone? What's next—watching my skills atrophy and drop off one by one? At what point will I become an invisible old woman? Am I there now? How did this happen? In my thirties, I climbed the thousand feet to the top of Camelback, my favorite Phoenix mountain, every Sunday morning, stopped for a minute at the summit, and hiked back down in an hour. I slipped down scree slopes just because it was the fastest way to the bottom. Is it time to say goodbye to the part of me who used to move with grace? Where did she go?

I realize that I am paralyzed with fear. The weight of it pins me to the floor. I am the woman stuck on the side of the mountain.

The day before we planned to go caving, Nick and I drove to the Forest Service office in Douglas on the Arizona/Mexico border to drop off the permission page and pick up the key. The Forest Service installed a locking metal gate at the entrance to the cave in the mid-1970s to protect the crystals that remained, an official example of too little, too late.

I handed a hundred-dollar bill to a woman behind a window in a tiny vestibule in the Forest Service office. As she handed me a receipt she warned, "Be sure to bring the key back within three days if you want your money back."

On our return to the research station we admired the passing landscape—scrub-covered mountains under skies that touched the horizon in all directions. About halfway back I caught sight of something out of the corner of my eye so strange I asked Nick to stop the van. We bushwhacked across the wide shoulder to find that a great horned owl had gotten so badly tangled in a barbed wire fence it was hanging upside down from a wing joint. It had been dead for some time. Up close it seemed so much smaller and less threatening than the powerful predator I knew it to be. A pair of great horned owls used to call some nights from the rooftop of my cabin in Sulphur Canyon. I would lie in bed and listen to them talk to each other in what seemed like an intimate conversation, marveling at their ability to be fierce and vulnerable at the same time. As Nick and I considered ways to free the owl, I scanned the field behind the fence line for any tall trees the owl might have called home. I saw only lovegrass and scattered saltbush, punctuated by an occasional cholla or sotol. In a landscape this open, the owl must have been hunting and so driven by hunger it got careless.

"It must have misjudged the location of the top wire in the dark," Nick said.

"I'm not so sure," I said, thinking of how deftly owls can navigate, especially in the dark. "We'll never know why it made its last mistake." We could feel Border Patrol watching us from their vehicles parked conspicuously on the top of a treeless hill as we struggled to extricate the owl's wing, which was pierced to the bone. Without tools, we could do nothing. "I'm sorry," I said to a world with one fewer owl. We left the carcass where we found it, dangling from a barb.

The next morning six of us drove a half mile up a graded dirt road, parked the van, and hiked up about a third of a mile along dry Crystal Creek. One part of the creek bed was obviously a waterfall during a spring generous with rain. We used our hands to mount the boulders. When we arrived at the entrance to the cave, Nick reached through a slot in the gate and fit the key inside the lock from the inside. Wide slots in the gate grant passage to the Townsend's big-eared bats that breed there in the summer months. A female bat bears one pup at a time. At birth, the pup falls into a membrane between the mother's legs. She hangs onto the pup for three days before she simply lets go, testing its ability to fly. Pups who master flying will join the colony to forage for tasty insects and live out their lives in community. Those who fall to the cave floor perish.

The gate creaked open. Nick locked it again from the inside, leaving the key in the lock. Once in the cave, we donned our headlamps and readjusted our backpacks. Because this was my only experience in a wild cave, I wasn't smart enough to be afraid.

Every time I move my head, I see shadows that my headlamp sets dancing. Forty-foot stalactites throw shade on the far side of the cavern, making it hard to discern concave from convex. In the stillness of the cave, I question what I cannot see even though it is right in front of me. How well do I decipher what happens in the dark? How much do I miss no matter how well it's illuminated?

I tell myself that here in this cave I am not falling behind. I have found my own river and am floating in its current, while life flows at its daily pace above me. Down here, the earth has less distance to travel as it spins. If I stay here long enough, maybe I will age more slowly. The realization that I am growing older by the minute comes as a surprise.

I lose track of time; I can't tell how long I have been sitting here. Eventually I become aware of a dim light growing brighter as it approaches from below. Steve has left the others and is returning to the chamber where I wait. He sits with me in silence a few minutes before saying, "I'm ready to go back up if you are."

For a moment I can't respond. When people want to help me, in my mind, it begs the question: Who do they want to help? Perhaps a better question is: Who do I become with help?

I turn to Steve. "I have to tell you that I am really scared. I'm afraid I can't get out of here." I swallow hard and stare at the precipice.

"I'll help you," Steve says. "You'll be fine."

I wobble to my feet and follow Steve to the boulders that lead up and out. "Just put one foot there and one hand here," he directs me. I throw one last look back into the cavern before reaching for his outstretched hand. This cave is just big enough to contain my fears as they are: constructions, projections, shadows. I can almost picture the river that washed through this cave, carving out space enough to sustain a flood of astonishment.

In the dim light of my headlamp, I can see clearly. I do as Steve instructs, being mindful of where I place my hands and feet. I take Steve's hand when he offers it. I test each foothold to see if my boot slips or finds purchase. I concentrate on my next move; I do not look up or down. I do not slip. For several minutes, I do not think. We reach the gate before I have time to be surprised that we have arrived. My eyes are slow to adjust as I step into the light and blink. When I find my voice, I say to Steve, "I was afraid I was tugging on you too hard. I was afraid I was going to pull you off your perch above me."

Steve says, "We're all afraid of something."

We hike back down from the cave to the research station. Steve lets me lead the way and I set a slow pace. My legs make their own decisions; muscle memory puts one foot in front of the other.

"My legs feel like rubber," Steve says.

My mouth is so dry I don't reply, but it comforts me to realize that he, too, feels the cave in his body. Or maybe he is just being kind. We reach the steep descent through the creek bed, and I use my hands to crab my way down. I move clumsily and apologize.

The air and the sun feel good on my skin. I wonder how long the others will stay in the cave. I can still see the excitement on Nick's face when he locked the gate behind us and adjusted his headlamp. I remember the anticipation of the day before, when I suggested we take my car to the office in Douglas, and Nick insisted on driving the van. When I offered to help pay for gas, he refused, saying it was the research station's van and they always pay for the gas. I recall my feeling of inadequacy—like what I had to give was too meager to be considered. Like my offers were nothing more than feathers hanging from barbed wire, blowing in the breeze.

Steve and I reach Herb Martyr Road; it's just another half mile of flat gravel road to the research station. I thank Steve for his help, and I mean it. When Steve says, "That wasn't so bad, was it?" I'm not sure if he means the climb out or my letting go, at least temporarily, of my tightly held independence, but either way, he is right.

When I look back over the trail we have just taken, I see the sun approaching the tops of the ponderosa pines against a faded sky. I hold my hand up to shield my eyes and see that the dust we are kicking up hangs suspended in the air. I breathe in the scent of the horehound growing along the road. In another half mile, I will drink deep from the water cooler in the dining room. I will unlace my hiking boots. It will be an hour or two before my legs stop shaking. Eventually I will wash the grit and dust off my hands and face and take a good look at myself in the mirror, wondering who I see there. I believe the woman looking back at me will continue to push her limits, although maybe not underground, in the dark, on the edge of a precipice.

The Gift of a Greyhound

I didn't administer the injection of the sedative that calmed him physically and mentally or the dose of pentobarbital that stopped his heart. But I had called the vet and scheduled the appointment. I emailed directions to my house and greeted the vet and the vet tech at the door. When the time came, I asked Dillon to lie down on his bed and go to sleep. Good dog that he was, he obeyed.

Before you drag out your hierarchy of griefs—nothing is worse than losing a child, or a spouse, or a parent—let me quote Cervantes, who knew something about the nobility of love. Comparisons are odious.

The thing about euthanasia is that you have to choose the day to do it. It's not the worst thing, obviously. The worst thing is that an animal you loved and cared for will be dead. And once you choose your day, and everyone plays their part, your decision is irreversible.

The other worst thing is flipping the switch from caregiver to lifetaker, from doing everything you can to keep the dog alive to choosing the hour he will take his last breath. I can quote all the platitudes about "if you love him, let him go" and "the greatest gift is the gift of freedom." But that's not the point. The question is *when*. Should tomorrow be the day he dies? Is he ready? Am I? Is that what he wants or am I just looking for convenience? Will I wait too long? Will I act too soon?

Dillon was a gift—a Christmas present from a friend when I moved to the Chiricahua Mountains. "To keep you company," my friend had said, "but you get to pick him out." My forty acres in Sulphur Canyon thick with jackrabbits, scaled quail, and prickly pear was a perfect place for a greyhound to stretch his legs, although an isolated spot for a human.

When I arrived at the greyhound rescue center in Sierra Vista, I walked between two long rows of kennels. Dog after dog watched me pass, with sad, pleading eyes or happy expectant faces or looks of desperate innocence. None had given up the hope of finding love.

Dillon wasn't my first choice—I had my eye on a handsome red male with a broken leg who reminded me of Phoenix, my first greyhound. Surely a veterinary surgeon could set the dog's leg and we would soon be taking long walks together through the arroyos. The woman from the adoption agency surprised me when she said that the dog needed rest and recuperation, not long walks in desert washes. She guided me past more dogs, beautiful greyhounds all, but none spoke to me in a way that tugged at my heart. Finally we reached the last cage, where a seventy-pound black male danced a happy dance at the sight of visitors. When I stepped inside his enclosure, he stood on his back toes and gracefully kissed my nose. The woman led him outside to a dog run, where he raced over the gravel with a generous enthusiasm. I was hesitant, not sure I could handle the dog's high energy and strong personality. "Does this dog smile?" I asked the woman, remembering Phoenix's goofy, toothy smile that even strangers found endearing. A greyhound's smile is just one more trait, along with their inability to sit and their powerful attachment to soft beds, that makes them special. "No," she replied with a deflated frown. I started to walk back to the gate when the dog ran up to me and pressed his body hard against my legs, stopping me in my tracks. "But he is a leaner," she said. "We call them Velcro dogs."

I reached down to pet the animal at my knees and was amazed at how warm he was—a black dog in the Arizona sun. He was also incredibly soft—softer than the most luxurious fur, and alive with a heartbeat that pulsed under my fingertips. His expression showed concern—fear—that I was going to leave him. "I'm right here," I whispered, stroking his side.

"Shame it's so hard to place a black dog. They tend to stay here the longest," the woman said.

"Why?" I asked.

"People want the fawns or the brindles—the pretty dogs," she said, watching me watching him. "This guy's name is Utah."

I'm a pushover for an underdog, especially one that's soft and warm. I signed the paperwork and paid the fees, but Utah wouldn't be mine for another couple of weeks—just enough time to think of a new name. My first greyhound was as red as Arizona sandstone, but "Sedona" was too feminine a name for a muscular male with thighs as sturdy as Easter hams. For Utah's new name, I studied a map of the four corner states. "Gallup" and "Durango" were easy to rule out, but "Winslow" and "Chama" were possibilities. I practiced calling "Kayenta" and "Ouray" out loud. Ultimately, Dillon was named after a reservoir west of Denver, although my literary friends who heard his name remained convinced Dillon was heir to a certain exuberant Welsh poet.

Our first rides in my SUV through winding canyon roads turned out to be early indicators of a delicate stomach; Dillon was vomiting before we were halfway through the switchbacks. We learned together; the first time Dillon saw a rabbit, he was on a leash. He lurched so suddenly I was afraid his neck would snap. He wore a halter from that time forward. He was walking on that halter when he spotted a coyote; he sprinted off at a flash that brought me to my knees and dragged me through a stand of prickly pear. It seemed silly to walk a dog on a leash on forty fenced acres, but I knew better than to let a sighthound trained to chase any moving thing run off leash through a desert with many distractions. He did, however, enjoy the enclosed yard off the kitchen. More than once he laid on the doorstep the crafty rabbit that managed to find a way through the double layer of wire mesh.

Before he retired, Dillon raced at Tucson Greyhound Park, a track with a reputation as the last chance for a downgraded dog. I don't know how long he raced, or how long he lived at the greyhound rescue facility, but he was almost four years old when I adopted him in 2005. A retired racing greyhound knows nothing about being a pet. Dillon learned quickly about mirrors and windows and stairs, but the concept of owning something, like a bed or a toy, proved trickier. He grew protective, piling his toys on a corner of his blanket for safekeeping.

I taught Dillon to play by grabbing his squeaky toy from his toy basket first thing every morning and running into the kitchen. He learned to chase me because he knew I would toss his toy to him, and he would catch it, and we would do it again until he stopped first, which he always did. He also learned that when he gave up the game, I would make his breakfast. I still don't know who trained whom.

On the track, greyhounds are fed 4D meat, which comes from livestock that is dead, down, diseased, or dying. They eat the meat raw, and when a hundred dogs in a kennel are waiting to be fed on a warm summer afternoon, the meat often sits unrefrigerated on an outside table for hours. You can't blame a greyhound for having an extremely sensitive digestive system. Aggravate that system with most packaged dog food, made from questionable ingredients at best or melamine and other tainted products at worst, and even the healthiest dog will revolt. I tried every expensive wet and dry dog food on the market, but Dillon was allergic to them all. Every night, he would run outside to get sick. Every morning, I donated another bag of organic, limited-ingredient dog food to the Cochise County Animal Hospital. After much trial and error, the diet he ultimately settled on consisted of a cup each of cooked ground beef, cooked potatoes or rice, grated raw carrots, and whatever other vegetable was in the refrigerator, usually green beans or peas. Four cups of food, twice a day. Although I hadn't eaten red meat in more than thirty years, I got a freezer and began buying and cooking ground beef by the case. People behind me in line at the supermarket checkout tried to guess what I was up to.

"Having a chili cook-off?" one couple asked. "Is it a hamburger party again tonight?" asked another.

"No," I would reply. "I have a greyhound."

Dillon didn't need to work very hard to earn his place in my heart. His endearing traits were many: His steadfastness. His seeming appreciation for the view into Sulphur Canyon. The love he had for his stuffed hedgehog. The kisses on my nose. The fact that he was soft and warm and would always be. And importantly, the trust and faith that glowed in his eyes each morning when we woke up and the first thing we saw was each other.

This is not another tear-jerker about a dying dog. This is about you, and it's about me. It's about the emotional logic that shifts in time of crisis, when you face a decision you can't avoid, and it's painful and unwelcome. It's about love.

When you adopt a dog, you know his shelf-life is shorter than yours. You know chances are good that you will either watch him die, or you'll turn away. Either way, his death is coming, and you'd better be prepared. That's part of the deal. But with his death comes a choice. You can decide that suffering, yours and his, is meaningless and realize only the pain. This is actually the harder choice. Or you can accept the challenge to transform tragedy into responsibility. If the death of your dog leaves you struggling for answers, maybe you're asking the wrong questions. Rather than questioning the meaning of death, try flipping it. Maybe it's life that is asking you for meaning.

Dillon was the second greyhound I lost to cancer. Like all racing greyhounds, Dillon's birthday was tattooed in his ear. If he had lived another three weeks, he would have turned 12. When he started vomiting again, I assumed he had found another dead bird under a bush or some other morsel on the desert floor. But this time he was having trouble breathing. An early morning visit to his vet brought the bad news I had been dreading as I watched Dillon age. His vet suspected lymphoma but recommended a specialist for confirmation. I couldn't get an appointment until the next day and spent a long, frightful night full of uncertainty. Dillon was panting and restless; I pulled some blankets and a pillow next to his bed and slept on the floor with one hand on his side, feeling the heartbeat that still pulsed under my fingertips. I'm right here, I said.

By the time I got to the specialty veterinary clinic the next afternoon, Dillon had grown seriously weak and dangerously thin. An x-ray revealed a mass the size of a grapefruit in his abdomen. An ultrasound showed that the tumor was related to lymphoma, which meant it was pointless to try to remove it. The internist gave me three choices. Chemotherapy would give him eight months to a year. Prednisone would buy about six to eight weeks. Or I could put him down.

Death and dying are two different animals. I knew his death was inevitable, but I wasn't prepared for the dying part. At what point did he stop living and start dying? When could I accept that there was no love strong enough to stop what was coming?

Chemotherapy was out of the question. Dillon threw up if I switched from carrots to corn; I could only imagine how sick he would get from chemo. And what was the point of delaying the inevitable and watching him suffer? I wondered out loud if I should skip straight to option 3. "Think positive," the internist said. "He could respond well to the Prednisone. Why don't you try it and see? Just be aware that it will make him very hungry."

On Prednisone, Dillon couldn't get enough food. We went from four cups of food twice a day to four cups three times a day and then to constant meals. He demanded food fifteen minutes after a full meal, and every fifteen minutes after that. Any objective other than eating became trivial. The one activity I thought he still enjoyed were our daily trips to the dog park.

In Santa Fe, where Dillon and I moved after I left Sulphur Canyon, the most typical relationship is a middle-aged woman and her dog. When I drove Dillon to the dog park, which I did every day regardless of snow, rain, heat, and wind, I felt I needed a vanity plate on my SUV that read "cliché." He rode in the back, barking at the horses that lived along the route. We used one of the individual dog runs, where I could let him off leash and he didn't have to worry about where I was or what I wanted from him. Mostly we each got lost in our own thoughts for an hour. But two weeks after his diagnosis, it was just too much. He entered the dog run, took a dump, and headed back to the gate, ready to go home.

What would you do if you knew this was your last week on earth? What do you do when you know that this is the last time you will curse the snow in your driveway, smell the coffee in the cup you raise to your lips, feel the sun on your skin? What makes each day special? By the time I realized that Dillon's days were numbered, he was too lethargic to do any of the things he used to enjoy. Note to self: Don't wait.

Prednisone transformed Dillon from a skeleton in a fur coat to a round roly-poly toy. I called his internist again. "He's eating so much his abdomen looks extended," I said. "But maybe it's the tumor. I can't tell."

"It sounds like he is extremely sensitive to steroids," the internist said.

"He's a greyhound," I wailed. "He's sensitive to everything."

"Try cutting the dose in half and see how he does. If that doesn't work, call me back."

"I can see that he's losing muscle mass in his shoulders and thighs. He looks like he's wasting away, except for his big round middle."

"That's the nature of this disease. Lymphoma is catabolic—the cells in the muscle tissue start to break down."

"This can't be healthy," I complained, aware of how crazy I sounded. I glanced over at Dillon, for the hundredth time that morning, as he stood in the sun near a window. His eyes seemed dimmed and his body sagged with profound sorrow. Or maybe it was my own sorrow that I was projecting onto him. "How much worse can this get?"

"You don't want to see how much worse it can get," the internist said. "Lymphoma can affect his kidneys and his liver. It can even go to his brain."

"I think it already has started to affect his brain. I often see him standing in the middle of the room, staring at the floor. Yesterday he was just standing in the kitchen, staring at his dinner bowl. When I said something to him, he jumped, like he was startled."

"It might be time to make some decisions. You might want to let him go with dignity."

What dies? What heals? I am defined by the existence of others, as night defines day, as death defines life. A profound sadness, an expansive joy, a hard-earned success, a devastating failure—all offer opportunities for introspection and growth. Teachers come in many forms. They can be your best friend or the most irritating pain in the ass. And sometimes they can be a dog.

The next afternoon when Dillon was his most restless, I sat on the floor next to his bed. He came to lie down by my side, reaching one paw out to touch my leg. I'm right here, I said. I scratched his ears and ran my hand over his bloated gut. I told him I loved him and always would, and that I never would forget him. I told him I forgave him for all the times he made me mad—for stealing that stick of butter off the counter after I left the kitchen, and for getting into the garbage that I forgot to put outside. I asked him to forgive me for the times I left him home alone too long when I knew he needed to go outside, or for leaving him alone at all. I gave him permission to go. But in my heart I was begging him to remove the responsibility for his death from me. I wanted him to die—I didn't want to have to put him down. As the hours stretched on, sitting on the floor, the unfairness of it all—the interdependence between us and our pets, the medical system that can prolong life without ensuring its quality, the burden of euthanasia— overwhelmed me. I began to sob uncontrollably, screaming at the dead air. "I don't want to do this, I can't do this, I don't want any part of it," I cried. "Tell me what to do," I pleaded. "Tell me something— anything."

The next morning I called his vet. "I feel like I'm waiting for something," I said. "Some kind of signal. The night before my first greyhound died from bone cancer, he was screaming in pain."

"That was a different kind of cancer," the vet explained. "Osteosarcoma is extremely painful, and that kind of pain is impossible to manage. Lymphoma is different. He won't be in that kind of pain."

"I don't know what to do."

"How is his quality of life?" his vet asked. I didn't know how to respond. How much suffering is enough? How much does it hurt and who hurts the most?

You will know when the time comes, my friends told me. He'll give you a sign, they said. They were wrong. The sign didn't come from him, but from deep inside me. As Dillon moved closer to death, I realized that I was trying to maintain control over how he suffered and how he died. I thought I could define what a "good death" looked like for him. By controlling his death, I was practicing controlling my own. The last gift he gave me was the knowledge that there is no such thing as a "good death," even though we hope that's what waits for us when our time comes. There's not even a "bad death"—there is just our death, and each one of us must do it our own way. Dillon's dying pulled me through the knothole of fear and uncertainty into a place filled with the courage to look straight at his death, and ultimately mine. What I found was a grace that appeared spontaneously in the pure lived moment.

When the time came, Dillon was the good dog he had always been. He put his head on the vet tech's lap while she prepared the two syringes. I sat on the floor, right in front of him, where he could see me easily. He never took his eyes from mine. He looked at me with eyes full of love and trust, deeper than imaginable. I sank into that infinite love, knowing it was the purest, most unadulterated gift. My heart filled with gratitude.

Dillon was the companion who would never lie to me or betray me. He greeted me at the door each time I came home, no matter how late, with an endless supply of kisses on my nose. He loved me with an undying love, and he would never leave me, until he did.

The vet injected the drugs, and Dillon sighed one deep sigh of acceptance—his last breath.

I'm right here.

I don't see Dillon anywhere. I miss him everywhere. Love is as strong as death.

A Chiricahua Glossary

Apache Wars. Forcible removal of the Chiricahua Apaches from their lands. My stone cabin at the mouth of Sulphur Canyon in southeastern Arizona was built in their ancestral home, although their homeland stretched across state and national borders. I was a guest on land that Chiricahua Apaches believe can never be owned by anyone.

Arroyo. Also known as a *wash*. A dry creek bed that fills with water during a flash flood, usually quickly and without warning. It's a dangerous situation that is getting worse as temperatures climb and storms intensify. (See *unprecedented*.)

Attention. A debt to be paid. In one of my favorite poems, "Sometimes," Mary Oliver writes:
"Instructions for living a life: / Pay attention./ Be astonished./ Tell about it."

Border. Delineate, dream, deny, exclude, entrap, in that order.

Canyon. Not even a canyon is permanent. In fact, it's a study in change—big change that takes a long, long time. Except, of course, the changes brought by the destruction we've caused in the last hundred years.

Cave Creek Canyon. The middle canyon in the Chiricahua Mountains, the most populated, the most famous. The canyon with all the tourists, who tend to be birders looking for trogons. See *Elegant Trogon* (if you're lucky).

Change. Unavoidable. I like to tell myself it won't ever come here, but I know better. It already has. See *Canyon*.

Chihuahua. The Mexican neighbor to the south. *Chee-WAH-wah*. Not to be confused with Chiricahua.

Chiricahua. A place and a language as well as a group of people. Most people stumble when pronouncing it for the first time. It's *cheer-eh-KAH-wa*.

Creosote. Ubiquitous shrub in the desert Southwest. Individual plants can live more than a hundred years; they can survive up to two years without water, a useful talent in a drought. Families of creosote plants grow by gradually expanding their circle of relatives, which eventually become their own individuals and start their own circles.

Cultural anthropologist. Nonnative PhD who tries to apply the logic of an outsider to a native belief system. Usually unwelcome at local parties.

Desert. A dry place. Some people describe it as an empty place, but they're just not paying close enough attention. The many types and classifications of deserts all share common characteristics. See *Dust*. (But keep your eyes closed.)

Dust. Everywhere.

Dust storm. Not a figure of speech.

Elegant Trogon. A sluggish, hunchbacked bird with metallic colors and a dog's bark. The male is bright red on his breast, brilliant green on his back, and copper on his long tail; the female is a drab metallic bronze. A specialty of southern Arizona.

Elevation. Not a measure of altitude, but a hierarchy of social order. The first question someone who lives in the Chiricahua Mountains asks a new resident: "So what's your elevation?" The higher your elevation, the more parties you are invited to. Unless you're a cultural anthropologist.

Extirpation. Often confused with extinction. Extirpation means that a species no longer exists at the local level. Extinction means the species no longer exists anywhere. If your favorite animal—pick one, there are several to choose from (gray wolf, masked bobwhite quail, Chiricahua leopard frog)—has been extirpated from your area, you can hope that a zoo somewhere in the world has developed a program to try to save the species.

Field guide. My most-studied books. When all my favorite plants and animals in my dog-eared field guides become extirpated or extinct, I can thumb fondly through the pages and reminisce. Or I can do something, anything, about it today.

Flash floods. Yes, they happen, and no, it doesn't need to be raining where you are. If you're standing in a dry wash and it's raining in the mountains above you, it's time to get to higher ground. Now. (See *arroyo*.)

Gegenschein. Sunlight bouncing off dust outside the atmosphere. The gegenschein is hard to see, but if I stand outside on a moonless fall night at midnight, point my face toward the heavens, and wait for my eyes to adjust, an oval of smudged light will appear just off the center of my vision. Just knowing that this smudge, slightly brighter than the surrounding dark sky, is composed of interplanetary detritus that has been drifting for millennia cheers me.

Gratitude. Giving thanks for a gift you don't have to return. Gratitude makes you more grateful. A byproduct of paying attention and noticing things, being open to the unknown.

Haboob. A lovely word for a dangerous wind that extends thousands of feet into the atmosphere and miles across the land. It heaves a wall of dust in your direction, visibility drops to zero, gusts burst to seventy miles an hour, and a bright day becomes a fuzzy nightmare.

Home. Where the heart is. Where you hang your hat. Where your family lives. Your natal place. A place you leave. A place I'm still looking for.

Hoodoo. A rock formation in the badlands. A geologic characteristic of the sky islands that are the Chiricahua Mountains, especially in the Chiricahua National Monument. The Chiricahua Apaches call them *standing rocks.* A word I love to say out loud. Hoodoo? You do?

Isolation. See *Loneliness.*

Jackrabbit. Two species of jackrabbits live in southern Arizona and New Mexico: the black-tailed jackrabbit (*Lepus californicus*) and the white-sided jackrabbit (*Lepus callotis*). I've seen plenty of black-tails but have never seen a white-sided jackrabbit. I've heard only about a hundred individuals remain in the wild.

Javelina. A peccary, not a pig. The collared peccary (*Tayassu tajacu*) is the species of javelina you can see in southeastern Arizona. A herd of javelinas is called a *squadron,* which is an arrangement they like to form close to your bird feeders. They recognize each other by their strong odor (and you will, too). Javelinas are not endangered and are not usually dangerous, unless you threaten them to stay away from your bird feeders.

Kangaroo rat. Neither a kangaroo nor a rat. Three species of kangaroo rats live in the desert southwest, and I have seen them all: Desert kangaroo rat (*Dipodomys deserti)*, Merriam's kangaroo rat (*D. merriami*), and banner-tailed kangaroo rat (*D. spectabilis*). A kangaroo rat's hearing is so good it can hear an approaching owl or snake. One more reason to respect a rat.

Keraunophobia. An abnormal fear of lightning and thunder. Symptoms include a keen interest in weather forecasts and a strong desire to take shelter from the storm. When a storm rumbles out of Sulphur Canyon, thunder echoes off the rock walls and lightning strikes close enough to remind me of the canyon's name. I have been known to exhibit these symptoms during spring storms.

Landscape. The visible, solid features of the surface of a place. Can also refer to the emotional environment that describes an individual's ups and down, peaks and arroyos.

Legacy. The memoir we leave behind for the next generation. What will remain if we destroy it all? What will we remember when there is no longer a point of reference?

Loneliness. Inevitable.

Love. A passion. I believe that you can fall in love with a mountain more easily than you can fall in love with a person. No. That's not right. No love is easy.

Mass wasting. A downward rockslide on an unstable slope. Human activity and excessive precipitation are the most common triggers. Studies of rock formation dynamics show that the landscape responds to stresses in its environment. A landslide in February 2001 closed a trail in the Chiricahua National Monument on the west side of the mountains for a year and a half. How much can a mountain take? How much can any of us endure?

Metamorph. One in transition, in the process of stepping into the unknown and becoming something else. Like a larva emerging from an egg, a Chiricahua leopard frog retaining its tail.

Monsoon season. The weeks from mid-June to late September when rain actually hits the ground in the Arizona desert instead of evaporating into mid-air. See *Virga.*

Mounds. Hard-to-define hillocks, tinier than a mountain, more indivi-dualistic than a hill, rounder than a peak, softer and more inviting than a tor. My mile-away neighbors call them The Three Gumdrops. I could see these mini-mounts from my kitchen window, where I greeted them most mornings with humility and gratitude.

Natural light. Piercing pastel in the mornings, slanted and gold hot in the afternoons. The kind of light I always knew was shining somewhere and that I found in Sulphur Canyon.

Neighbors. Miles away. Learn to like them all because the day will come when you will need them or they will need you. A day might even come when you will simultaneously need each other. That will be a day to be thankful for.

Opuntia. Prickly pear. The "prickly" part is perfect but the "pear" part is perverse.

Parthenogenesis. Reproduction that does not require sex. A real-life form of virgin birth. There are as many types of parthenogenesis as there are sexual positions, but most types involve females who produce clones. Practiced locally by whiptail lizards.

Pavement. Not in Sulphur Canyon. Only one paved road, Portal Road, leads into or out of the eastern slope of the Chiricahua Mountains. Dirt roads in the Chiricahuas are so dry-packed they feel paved—until the monsoons come.

Petrichor. The smell of rain in the desert. From the Greek word *petra*, "rock," and *ichor*, "blood of the gods." An extirpated term that might soon become extinct.

Portal. A community in Cave Creek Canyon. Population estimates vary from 90 to 150, depending on your attitude toward borders. A portal is also an entrance, a launching point, an invitation to explore. What you discover when you pass through a portal is up to you.

Rain. An occurrence and a resource people in the desert pray for. Our prayers are answered only occasionally, and lately hardly at all.

Rattlesnake. A pit viper. Thirteen known species of rattlesnakes in the world are native to Arizona (I have seen six of them): Mohave. Western diamondback. Western. Black. Black-tailed. Banded rock. Twin-spotted. Ridge-nosed. Prairie. Massasauga. Sidewinder. Speckled. Tiger.

Rhyolite. The rock type that gives the Chiricahua Mountains their distinctive pinkish-grey color. Rhyolite that cools too quickly grows crystals that form obsidian, a glassy, jet-black, stronger-than-glass rock called "Apache tears" by nonnative people who prefer maudlin myths to the history of grief.

Saguaros. Don't grow here. See Tucson. That is, drive to Tucson and open your eyes.

Scorpion. A tiny, pale monster with lobster claws and a tail that curves over its back and ends with a venomous stinger. You can find them if you shine an ultraviolet light outside at night. You can also find them by picking up rocks. Be sure to wear gloves.

Sotol (*Dasylirion wheeleri*). An agave-like plant in the asparagus family. The name comes from the Nahuatl word *Tzotolin* meaning "palm with long and thin leaves." *Sotoleros* make an alcoholic drink from the fermented hearts of the plants; sotol is said to taste like its specific terroir, with hints of the plant's struggle to survive in a desert with poor soil and not enough rain.

Speciesism. Mankind's assumption of superiority that manifests in our exploitation of animals.

Stars. More than I will ever know.

Tumbleweed. A strategy for dispersal used by opportunistic weeds. A technique used by species that prefer disturbances. A method of breaking free and giving over to the whims of a passing wind.

Unprecedented. A word that no longer has meaning in a time of accelerating change. We have pushed the planet beyond its limits; there is no road map for this uncharted territory. But there are other words: *code red, consequences, catastrophic.*

Virga. Rain that evaporates before it hits the ground. Streaks of moisture hanging from the underside of a cloud on a desert horizon, suspended like whispered prayers.

Wall. A border we build around ourselves for protection, which serves to seclude as well as isolate. A self-made prison. Something meant for climbing.

Walmart. Portal's closest store (fifty-five miles away in Douglas, Arizona), where you can buy a variety of goods. Specialties include Pampers, Nescafé, and six types of bottled sotol.

Water. The most important thing in the desert, and like love, there's not enough of it.

Wind. Constant.

Xeriscaping. Gardening with little or no water. Get used to it.

Yucca. A spiky desert plant with more than forty different species. *Yucca gloriosa*, also called *Spanish dagger*, is known for its rapier-like leaf tips that grow at shin level.

Zilch. Nada, goose egg, diddly squat. What I knew about life in the desert before moving to the Chiricahuas.

Zillions. The number of discoveries still awaiting me.

Notes on the essays

My deep appreciation extends to the Chiricahua Apaches and all indigenous people who lived in these mountains. The essays in this book take place on land that is the ancestral homeland of the Ndé, particularly the Chiricahua Apache people. Gratitude as well to my neighbors, past and present, human and nonhuman, who have spent their lives here. My heart goes out to all those who walk this land.

I consulted many books and other reference material while working on these essays, including dictionaries and Wikipedia. Some of the general knowledge that found its way into this book was sourced from *Cave Creek Canyon: Revealing the Heart of Arizona's Chiricahua Mountains* (New Mexico: ECO Publishing, 2019), an enlightening anthology edited by Wynne Brown and Reed Peters.

A big thank you to the New Mexico Writers for the 2021 Douglas Preston Travel Grant award, which funded some of the in-person research done for this book. Thank you also to Storyknife for giving me the gift of time to work on the final edits.

Special thanks to Doug Carlson, Andre Dubus III, Camille Dungy, Allen Gee, Renny Golden, Sean Hill, Pam Houston, Susan Fox Rogers, Heidi Schulman, Mary Sojourner, and Joni Tevis for their close reads and helpful feedback.

And a huge heartfelt thank you to Donald L. Jordan for establishing *The Nature Series at DLJ Books* and for giving *Mountain Time* such a welcome home.

Mountain Time

John Moriarty wrote about God and mountains and many other things in *Nostos: An Autobiography* (Dublin, The Lilliput Press, 2001), which has been described by one reviewer as a "long slog" of a book. Well worth reading, and you don't have to slog to the end.

You can listen to John O'Donohue talk about landscape and the Irish imagination on "Longing and Belonging: The Complete John O'Donohue Audio Collection" (Sounds True, 2012). You can hear John O'Donohue discuss the Inner Landscape of Beauty with Krista Tippett at On Being: https://onbeing.org/programs/john-odonohue-the-inner-landscape-of-beauty/

My research into my Kerry grandparents led me to Agnes O'Sullivan of Taobh Coille in Kells, to whom I am grateful for her encouragement and hospitality.

I gathered much information about An Gorta Mór from *The Great Hunger: The Story of the Potato Famine of the 1840s which killed one million Irish peasants and sent hundreds of thousands to the new world* by Cecil Woodham-Smith. (London: Penguin, 1991).

Bought and Sold: A History of Lies and Broken Promises

My first round of thanks goes to Hattie Fletcher for her close read and superb edits when preparing this essay for life as a *True Story* from *Creative Nonfiction Magazine*. Shout out also to Chad Vogler for his meticulous fact checking and to the rest of the team at *True Story*. Thank you for keeping me honest.

Thank you to Bill Tooahyaysay Bradford and Joe Saenz for their generosity in sharing information with me about Chiricahua Apaches.

I still have the advertising "literature" and letters regarding the Deming Ranchettes that were in my father's possession when he died. Other section headings come from the online sources noted. Additional sources used in this essay include the City of Deming Downtown Master Plan developed in 2013; the City of Deming, New Mexico website; and the Luna County Museum, Deming, New Mexico.

You can see a copy of the photograph of Jefferson Davis and his family and servant at the Library of Congress: https://www.loc.gov/resource/ppmsca.23869/. You can find the names and ages of the men, women, and children sold at auction at the estate sale of James Gadsden in a document named "Another Weeping Time: Sale of 235 Slaves of Gen. James Gadsden, SC, 1860" at fold3.com.

For much of the background on New Mexico politics in the late 1800s, I relied on a paper by David Correia titled, "'Retribution Will Be Their Reward': New Mexico's Las Gorras Blancas and the Fight for the Las Vegas Land Grant Commons," published in Issue 108 (Fall 2010) of the *Radical History Review*. New Mexico History State Records and Archives (newmexicohistory.org) has more information on land grants in New Mexico. "Land-Stealing in New Mexico" by George W. Julian (*The North American Review*, Vol. 145, No. 368 (July, 1887) summed up the "'earth-hunger' in New Mexico, and the power of these grant owners." "Land-Grant Railroads and their Relation to Government Transportation: A Lecture Delivered Before the Officers of the Quartermaster Reserve Corps at Washington, D.C., June 26, 1917" by Maj. Robert E. Shannon, Quartermaster Reserve Corps, was especially enlightening. The New Mexico Office of the State Historian has a record of the colorful speech made by Pablo Herrera, who preferred spending time in the penitentiary over serving time in the New Mexico legislature. There are many more stories about the Santa Fe Ring, common use land, and the politics of the New Mexico Territory that you can find easily with a little bit of digging.

Much has been written about Cochise and George Bascom and the Chiricahua Apaches during the Indian War years—much of it conflicting. I relied on information from Edwin R. Sweeney, an authoritative biographer of Cochise and Mangas Coloradas, to set the record straight. His book *From Cochise to Geronimo: The Chiricahua Apaches 1874-1886* was especially helpful. Sweeney gives an account of the conversation between Cochise and Captain Frank Perry in his book *Cochise: Chiricahua Apache Chief* (Norman: University of Oklahoma Press, 1991).

In his orders to army commanders at Fort Bowie, President Grover Cleveland instructed, "All the hostiles should be very safely kept as prisoners until they can be tried for their crimes, or otherwise disposed of, and those to be sent to Florida should be started immediately." Telegrams between Cleveland and R.C. Drum, Acting Secretary of War, are recorded in The Executive Documents of the Senate of the United States for the Second Session of the Forty-ninth Congress, 1880-87. *From Fort Marion to Fort Sill* by Alicia Delgadillo and Miriam A. Perrett (Lincoln: University of Nebraska Press, 2013) detailed living conditions for Chiricahua Apache prisoners of war at Fort Marion from 1886 to 1913. An additional source was "Indian Claims in the Courts of the Conqueror" by Nell Jessup Newton (*The American University Law Review* [Vol. 41:753]).

Facts pertaining to the Chicago riots come from the Washington Post, April 15, 1968 and the Chicago Tribune, 1968. You can find a copy of the 1968 report to the National Commission on the Causes and Prevention of Violence at the US Department of Justice Office of Justice Programs. You can watch videos of the "police riot" outside the Democratic National Convention and watch Mayor Richard J. Daley issue his shoot-to-kill order on YouTube.

Quotes from Regis Pecos, former Cochiti Pueblo governor, come from a paper he wrote titled "The History of Cochiti Lake from the Pueblo Perspective," reprinted in the *Natural Resources Journal*, Volume 47, Summer 2007.

I found a copy of the 1978 Final Report of the Indian Claims Commission published online by the National Indian Law Library.

There is so much more historical background to these stories. I suggest doing your own research on the Treaty of Guadalupe Hidalgo, the Garay Project, the Isthmus of Tehuantepec, the Mexican-American War, and Thomas C. Durant. Also look into the westward expansion of the railroads, including the Pacific Rail Act of 1864, Section 2, which says, "The United States shall extinguish as rapidly as may be the Indian titles to all lands falling under the operation of this act, and required for the said right of way and grants hereinafter made."

I also suggest that non-Native people support indigenous communities in their area and upon whose land they live. Non-Native people can show their support by reading history told from a Native point of view as well as learning what Native-led organizations and nonprofits operate in their areas.

How Much Can a Bag Hold?

For this essay, I concentrated on immigration statistics from 2004-2006, the years I lived in Sulphur Canyon. I consulted a report from the United States Government Accountability Office written in August 2006 titled "Illegal Immigration: Border-Crossing Deaths Have Doubled Since 1995; Border Patrol's Efforts to Prevent Deaths Have Not Been Fully Evaluated." More information came from "Border Security: The Role of the U.S. Border Patrol," a Congressional Research Service Report for Congress by Blas Nuñez-Neto updated in May 2005.

How Far Would You Go to Save a Rat?

You can read more about pack rats and their middens in "50,000 years of vegetation and climate history on the Colorado Plateau, Utah and Arizona, USA" by Larry L. Coats, Kenneth L. Cole, and Jim I. Mead, and "USGS/NOAA North American Packrat Midden Database"; both are USGS publications.

You can learn about the research and listen to lab rats giggling while being tickled at: https://www.scientificamerican.com/article/ rats-enjoy-being-tickled-when-they-re-in-the-right-mood-video/

Hammer Test

A big debt of gratitude to Geoff Bender, Director of the Southwestern Research Station, for connecting me with the two men (who have asked to remain nameless) working to restore Chiricahua leopard frogs to the Chiricahua Mountains. Thanks also to Hunter McCall, who allowed me to tag along on his leopard frog surveys, and to Reed Peters, who showed me my first Chiricahua leopard frog at Cave Creek Ranch. And special thanks to Vickie Clancy for feeding me and making me feel at home.

The statistics about the extinction and decline of amphibian species caused by Bd come from an abstract from the Eastern Washington University's Student Research & Creative Works Symposium held in 2023 and published online. The quote about the scale of the threat of amphibian chytrid fungus was published in a paper from the Ecological Society of America (https://esajournals.onlinelibrary.wiley.com/doi/full/10.1002/eap.2724). You can find the paper from The Ecological Society of America in *Ecological Applications 33*(1): e2724. https://doi.org/10.1002/eap.2724.

The Nature of Mutability

My sincere thanks to Jim Frank Cox, who passed away at age 81 a little more than a year after we sat at his kitchen table at the base of the Sanford mound. You can hear him tell his stories in his gravelly voice in the archives of the Arizona Memory Project at the Arizona State Library. Thanks also to Ted Troller for his insights on ranching in the San Simon Valley. Special thanks to Bill Cavaliere for introducing me to his two friends, for reading a draft of this essay, and for all the hospitality in Portal.

Doug Ruppel, Douglas District Ranger, USDA Forest Service, Douglas, AZ graciously answered my questions about Lehmann lovegrass.

The quote about city slickers who drive recreational vehicles and join the Sierra Club is from the web page "Introduced Forages-Grasses –IB" written by R.E. Rosiere, Professor of Range Management, Tarleton State University, Texas A&M University System. http://range.altervista.org/Grasslands/introducedforages-grasses-ib.htm

Research material for this essay included "History, Status and Management of Lehmann Lovegrass" by Noelle Humphrey, published in *Rangelands* 16(5), October 1994, and "Lehmann Lovegrass—Central

South Africa and Arizona, USA" by Jerry R. Cox, G.B. Ruyle, Jan H. Fourle, and Charlie Donaldson, published in *Rangelands* 10(20), April 1988. I also read "Lehmann Lovegrass (*Eragrostis Lehmanniana Nees*) Annotated Bibliography" by Richard Chasey (6/1/2010) published by the Audubon Research Ranch.

Information about the history of cattle ranching in Arizona came from, among other sources, "Development of the Cattle Industry in Southern Arizona, 1870' and 80's" by J.J. Wagoner, "Early History of the Cattle Industry in Arizona," by Bert Haskett, "History of the Cattle Industry in the Southwest," by Clara M. Love, and "The Introduction of Cattle into Colonial North America," by G. A. Bowling. For a personal account of the "emergency" of the destruction of grazing land in the San Simon Valley from 1882 to 1935, read "Herds in San Simon Valley: What Has Happened to the Promised Land of Arizona's Oldtime Cattlemen" by Will C. Barnes, published by the University of Arizona.

The world's population was 1.6 billion in 1990; by 2000 it was 6.1 billion. Twenty years later it hit the 8 billion mark. You can read more statistics at the United Nations Population Fund and at the United States Census Bureau websites.

One Creature Among Many
A tip of my hat to Dr. Howard Topoff for showing me his ants, answering my questions, and reading a draft of this essay to catch any inaccuracies.

The majority of the background information in this essay came from *The Ants* by Bert Hölldobler and E. O. Wilson (Cambridge: Harvard University Press, 1990) and other papers, several by Howard Topoff, on the topic of slave-making ants.

My Eight-Snake Day
Thanks to Barney Tomberlin for collecting the Mohave rattlesnake from my yard. Barney was loved and respected in Portal, where he lived from the 1980s until his death on May 1, 2021.

Thanks as well to Bill Cavaliere for running my snake facts past Kevin Bowler, his resident snake expert.

Details about populations of the New Mexico Ridgenose Rattlesnake in the Animas Mountains come from the 1985 New Mexico Ridgenose Rattlesnake Recovery Plan prepared by Dr. Willian H. Baltosser and Dr. John P. Hubbard, Endangered Species Division, New Mexico Department of Game and Fish, Santa Fe, New Mexico.

Quotes from *The Little Prince* by Antoine de Saint-Exupéry come from a book I have had for years. Harcourt Brace Jovanovich, 1943, translated by Katherine Woods.

What Bluebirds Taught Me About Motherhood

Thank you to Robin (yes, that really was her name) from the Cornell Lab of Ornithology, who patiently answered my frantic questions about the behavior of nesting female Western bluebirds.

Statistical information about the conservation status of Western Bluebirds and other species mentioned in these essays comes from the International Union for Conservation of Nature (IUCN).

What the Two Percent Are Saying

Thank you to Dr. Con Slobodchikoff at Northern Arizona University for decades of research on prairie dogs, and for sharing knowledge with a yaprat like me. When I started learning about prairie dogs, I knew next to nothing about them. What I've learned leaves me with more questions than answers, like this one: What would you spend your precious days talking about if you realized your time left on the planet grew shorter with every breath?

Thank you as well to all the volunteers and other prairie dog friends who have worked so hard to keep prairie dogs alive and safe. A little research can turn up details too gruesome to mention about Red Mist Societies and other enemies of prairie dogs.

Time Passes like Water

The quote from Michel de Montaigne comes from his essay "On Fear," available in *Essays of Montaigne, Vol. 1*, 17th century English translation by Charles Cotton.

Franklin D. Roosevelt delivered his famous quote about fear during his 1933 inaugural address. A copy of his speech is available from the Franklin D. Roosevelt Presidential Library and Museum.

The Gift of a Greyhound

Joan Eidinger worked to end greyhound racing for fifteen years from her kitchen table in Phoenix, Arizona. I had the privilege of editing her newsletter, *Greyhound Network News*, until shortly before her death in 2018. I learned so much from Joan, and greyhound lovers worldwide owe her our gratitude.

A Chiricahua Glossary

The quote from Mary Oliver comes from her poem "Sometimes," published in *Red Bird* (Boston: Beacon Press, 2008). This book also includes the poem "Straight Talk from Fox": "Don't think I haven't / peeked into windows. I see you in all your seasons / making love, arguing, talking about God / as if he were an idea instead of the grass, / instead of the stars, the rabbit caught / in one good teeth-whacking hit and brought / home to the den. What I am, and I know it, is / responsible, joyful, thankful. I would not/ give my life for a thousand of yours."

There are many places to learn more about gegenschein. Good places to start are earthsky.org and science.nasa.gov.

The humanistic psychologist Abraham Maslow defined profound perceptions of reality as "peak experiences," which can infuse an ordinary activity with intense moments of self-awareness. His quote about perception comes from his essay titled "Religions, Values, and Peak-Experiences" (New York: Viking Compass Edition, 1970).

I still hope to see a white-sided jackrabbit in the bootheel. You can learn more about them in Aldo Leopold's book *Wildlife of Mexico: The Game Birds and Mammals* (California, University of California Press, 1959).

Acknowledgments

Essays from this collection have been published in the following literary journals or anthologies; a big debt of gratitude to all these publishers for giving my essays their first homes:

"Mountain Time" in *Border Crossing*, edited by Mary McMyne

"Bought and Sold: A History of Lies and Broken Promises" in *True Story* from *Creative Nonfiction*, edited by Hattie Fletcher

"How Much Can a Bag Hold" in the "Dignity as an Endangered Species" issue of *About Place Journal*, edited by Pamela Uschuk

"Hammer Test" in *River Teeth*, edited by Todd McKinney

"What Bluebirds Taught Me About Motherhood" in the anthology *When Birds Are Near,* from Cornell University Press, edited by Susan Fox Rogers

"What the Two Percent Are Saying" in *Muse/A Journal*, edited by Gregg Murray

"Time Passes Like Water" in the "Moxie" issue of *Chautauqua*, edited by Kenneth Matthew Thies

About the author

Renata Golden has studied the natural world in Arizona and New Mexico for decades. Her essays have been published in *Border Crossing, Creative Nonfiction, About Place Journal, River Teeth, Chautauqua,* and many other literary journals. Her work has been anthologized in *Dawn Songs: A Birdwatcher's Field Guide to the Poetics of Migration* by Talking Waters Press; *First and Wildest: The Gila Wilderness at 100* by Torrey House Press; and *When Birds Are Near* from Cornell University Press. She's been awarded a New Mexico Writers Douglas Preston travel grant and has held residencies at Storyknife and Write on Door County. Renata earned an M.F.A. from the University of Houston. Originally from the South Side of Chicago, she now lives in the shadow of the Sangre de Cristo Mountains in Santa Fe, New Mexico.

The Donald L. Jordan Endowment was established in 2016, in part, to facilitate the formation of Columbus State University Press, which was officially formed in 2021. CSU Press is pleased to recognize Mr. Jordan as the founder of the press, which serves as the publishing venue for the Donald L. Jordan Prize for Literary Excellence, and for The Nature Series at DLJ Books. DLJ Books has been installed as a permanent imprint at the press. Mr. Jordan's foresight made CSU Press a reality, and we are grateful for his generosity. Mr. Jordan passed away on May 15, 2023 after a very successful business career. The author of literary novels, short stories, and works of non-fiction, he was also particularly interested in helping other writers attain publication.